Marketing Your Consulting and Professional Services

Marketing Your Consulting and Professional Services

RICHARD A. CONNOR, JR. JEFFREY P. DAVIDSON

JOHN WILEY & SONS
New York • Chichester • Brisbane • Toronto • Singapore

ISBN 0-471-81827-5

Printed in the United States of America

10 9 8 7 6 5 4

This book is dedicated to

Emanuel Davidson

who knew full well
of its creation
years before its authors
and to

Susan

who supported me
during the
formative years

PREFACE

Marketing is an idea whose time has come to professional service firms.

This book gets right to the point. The text is concise, and we rely on exhibits that can be completed quickly and used on a daily basis. The exhibits also indicate various action steps available. The book has been prepared for the busy professional who has only basic-level knowledge of marketing and promotion or needs to bolster a "rusty" marketing perspective.

The central theme is the use of *leverage* to produce results. "Leveraging," as described by the authors, "is concentrating on the *smallest* number of clients, markets, and targets that will produce the *largest* amount of *profitable* revenue."

The book presents a "client-centered" view of marketing which was introduced by the senior author in 1969. Such a view makes your clients and targets the focus and beneficiary of your time and talents. This is in direct contrast to a firm-centered approach, which focuses on the marketing goals of the firm.

The techniques and recommendations presented here have proved effective for hundreds of professional service firms over the past 14 years, and if properly followed will work for any firm.

This book is designed to aid two groups. The first group consists of professional service providers and consultants who have little training in marketing and promotion, or who have been in practice for only a few years. The second group consists of those who have had some formal marketing instruction or are familiar with marketing principles as a result of their several years in practice and recognize that their prosperity and viability depend on an effective marketing plan.

This book offers such a plan. You will gain an understanding of the client-centered marketing approach, use of leveraging, and use of marketing and promotional tools in support of the client-centered approach.

In preparing the book, the authors—management consultants with over 350 articles published between them—have captured the essence of what is necessary to painlessly but effectively market professional services. We are greatly enthusiastic about the results this book can offer you, while recognizing how difficult it is for the busy professional to restructure thoughts, plans, and patterns of behavior. Accordingly, we have sequentially presented the material in this book so that on conclusion you will indeed be able to prepare your own client-centered marketing plan.

Research on learning effectiveness has shown that readers absorb more and are better satisfied with their learning when authors spell out what they are expected to know as a result of finishing each chapter and are given the opportunity to practice this knowledge. This focus has been kept in mind in developing each chapter.

This book consists of four sections, including a total of 21 chapters. The chapters are relatively self-contained to enable the reader to concentrate on specific subject areas. The purpose of each chapter and major questions addressed are presented as a prelude to the chapter that follows. Chapters also contain readily usable charts and checklists to aid you in putting a handle on, and finally mastering, the elements of an effective marketing plan.

In reading this book and adopting a client-centered marketing approach, we encourage you to do more than just one reading. We suggest a quick reading of the text the first time with attention to the charts but not a detailed review of every item. Detailed study is reserved for the second reading, in which you should slowly read, absorb, and follow through on the material presented.

We acknowledge the contribution of Rose Bravo, whose speedy fingers and even speedier mind made preparation of the manuscript a pleasure.

RICHARD A. CONNOR, JR.   JEFFREY P. DAVIDSON

January 1985

SOME PRACTICAL HINTS

The following practical hints are offered to aid the reader in successful implementation of the material presented.

1. Find a quiet place to read and get in the habit of going there to read the book.
2. Have plenty of scratch paper and a calculator.
3. Make up a schedule that includes time to work on your marketing plan, and stick to it. Regular effective market planning two or three times a week is much more effective than one long stretch.
4. Time yourself on breaks to make sure you are not getting sidetracked too much. It's a good idea to take a 5- to 10-minute break each hour rather than read for a long period of time.

CONTENTS

xiii

Marketing Your
Consulting and
Professional Services

PART

1

CLIENT-CENTERED
MARKETING

PROFESSIONAL SERVICE firms, once virtually immune to and protected from "distasteful" practices such as promotion and personal selling, must now operate in an environment that is characterized by rampant commercialism and impacted by rapid and radical changes.

We have found that the most successful professional service firms across a vast array of industries have geared their practice toward the needs of the client and primary market, as opposed to offering those services that the professional happens to be good at or can readily provide. We have termed this approach to marketing professional and consulting services *client-centered marketing*.

Client-centered marketing necessitates continual relationship development. All the professional's experience, planning, and action are targeted toward the needs of the client.

A *client-centered orientation* reduces the need for individual professionals to acquire and employ sophisticated and aggressive personal selling skills and expensive sales supports. The professional's goal is to mentally sit on the client's side of the desk to view the client's operations and needs through objective eyes. Thus the professional is able to identify ways to assist the client in doing better what the client is in business to do. This is really an advocate-oriented relationship.

Part 1, consisting of Chapters 1 through 8, introduces and explains the client-centered marketing approach, how to assess one's current status, the use of leveraging, cultivation of referrals, and prospecting.

After you complete Part 1 we believe your approach to marketing your service may change radically. The sections that follow will then provide you with the tools for marketing success.

THE CLIENT-CENTERED MARKETING APPROACH

CLIENT-CENTERED marketing refers to organized and coordinated activities designed to develop and enhance relationships and manage the firm's *image* with clients and other receptive and influential people. These clients and other people are or can be interested in using, retaining, and referring the firm and its services if you sense, serve, and satisfy their needs and expectations. After reading this chapter and slowly digesting it, you should be able to:

- ☐ Name four marketing objectives that can be achieved through a client-centered marketing program.
- ☐ Briefly explain how client-centered marketing differs from the "traditional" and "hard-sell" marketing approaches.
- ☐ Define leveraging in your own terms and in one sentence.
- ☐ Answer this question: "If clients don't purchase services, what do they purchase?"

MARKETING OBJECTIVES

Several major marketing objectives can be accomplished through a client-centered marketing program, including:

- ☐ Retaining key clients.
- ☐ Expanding services to existing clients.
- ☐ Upgrading or replacing marginal clients.
- ☐ Managing your image with clients and targets.
- ☐ Generating controlled, profitable growth.
- ☐ Offering services designed to satisfy the needs and expectations of clients and prospective clients.
- ☐ Attracting desirable prospective clients.

CLIENT-CENTERED MARKETING VERSUS OTHER APPROACHES

To understand why a client-centered marketing approach is stressed, it is helpful to contrast it with two other major approaches to marketing available to the professional—the traditional and the hard sell.

The *traditional* approach is basically a reactive one. The underlying assumption is that growth is solely the result of providing good technical services and meeting the existing demands of the marketplace. Thus encouragement of growth involves very little strategy or coordination of effort.

It's been said that "Doing what you've always done will get you what you've always gotten." Adherence to the traditional marketing orientation—waiting for the client to contact the professional on recognition of a need or problem—will seldom produce the additional new business required in today's intensely competitive situation. Too often a second, more aggressive firm is working to be next in line if you fail to anticipate needs.

Existing client problems are dealt with as they arise and are brought to the attention of the professional. Often, it is too late or too expensive to correct these problems and the disappointed client is inclined to replace the firm or cut back on the amount of additional work authorized. Usually, no organized prospecting programs for attracting eligible potential clients have been developed since referrals are taken for granted as the result of "doing a good job." In today's competitive market, these assumptions can be very costly.

The second traditional approach is known as the *hard sell*. Those following the hard-sell approach focus on getting out and getting known in their practice areas. Instead of focusing on client needs, they place the emphasis on "our firm," "our services," and "our reputation," assuming that growth is largely the result of being known in the community. This approach can be successful in the short run, since it will attract some "price-sensitive" clients looking for a "good deal."

The hard-sell approach has two major drawbacks. Some of the new business is questionable in terms of real and lasting value since these same clients may "shop" elsewhere later and also because quality clients eventually tire of an approach that is not sensitive to their needs.

An audit services firm instituted a hard-sell approach that involved contacting influentials such as lending officers, prominent attorneys, and others and soliciting referrals from them. Monthly goals were set for each of the partners and managers by the partner in charge. After several months the program "died" an obscure death. Several years later the partner in charge was still wondering why his troops didn't "see the light."

LEVERAGING

The notion of leveraging is integral to effective client-centered marketing. The dictionary defines leverage as "the advantage or gained power from an action." In marketing terms, leveraging is the process of identifying and capitalizing on the *smallest* number of actions that produce the *greatest* results.

Leveraging the time of your staff and other scarce and costly resources is essential. Your firm's primary task is to sense, serve, and satisfy the needs of its clients at a reasonable profit while handling an increasingly expanding "pending actions" list. You need to make certain that every minute devoted to marketing counts.

MARKETING IN PERSPECTIVE

Our experience in working with or speaking before professional service firms in many segments indicates that without major program status, marketing is seldom effective and long-lasting.

A successful professional practice can be compared with a balanced four-legged stool:

Leg 1 is technical quality: consistent, superb service delivered on a timely basis.

Leg 2 is personnel: selecting, training, developing, motivating, and retaining the best staff available.

Leg 3 is financial administration.

Leg 4 is client-centered marketing: sensing, serving, and satisfying the needs of present and potential clients to provide the best services available.

Client-centered marketing is essentially relationship development, and the relationship is based on a complex array of technical and personal factors that create a high degree of interdependence. The client is the target and the beneficiary of all the professional's experience, planning, and actions.

Professionals who are effective in marketing have learned along the way to develop relationships with those clients and others who are readily willing and able to assist them in their various marketing and selling activities. They search constantly for the relatively few key contacts who facilitate leveraging of resources, to achieve results with the minimum expenditure of time and energy. In short, you must recognize the fact that not all clients are created equally.

Effective client-centered marketing requires acknowledgement that:

1. Clients don't purchase services, but rather purchase your promise to produce a more favorable future for them on schedule, within budget, and in a manner that meets their expectations. One exceptionally able professional made it a practice to surface the client's expectations regarding the final product or "deliverable" by asking the question: "How will you and I know when I'm doing the job you expect me to?" The answer to this question invariably surfaces both reasonable and unrealistic expectations that need to be negotiated.

2. Services are really "bought" or rejected in the "gut" by clients, and the decision is justified to themselves and others by the use of hard copy such as proposals and testimonials.

3. Value is always defined by the recipient, not the provider. It is always rooted in one's needs system. Value is a function of one's needs being identified and satisfied in ways that meet one's expectations.

This chapter has introduced client-centered marketing, defined leveraging, and provided the foundation for the client centered marketing model discussed in Chapter 2.

2

THE CLIENT-CENTERED MARKETING MODEL

FOUR ELEMENTS comprise the client-centered marketing model and we describe each of them in this chapter. Completion of this chapter will enable you to:

☐ Cite benefits that clients seek as a result of your services.

☐ In your marketing effort, determine why it is more important and effective for you to identify specific need situations of clients and to relate and discuss relevant benefits than to simply present your firm's services and capabilities.

ELEMENTS OF THE MARKETING MODEL

The four major elements to the marketing model include:

- ☐ Performance
- ☐ Referrals
- ☐ Targets
- ☐ Promotion

The *performance* element focuses on several aspects of an existing professional practice:

1. The recent *financial* growth in terms of fee, volume, and billable hours.
2. *Existing clients* and the potential they represent for growth and problems.
3. *Existing markets* and the potential they represent for growth and competition.
4. *Existing services* and their degree of client-centeredness and "cutting edge."

The second model element is *referrals*. There are two classes of referrals:

1. *Clients* who refer your firm to others.
2. *Nonclients* such as bankers and association executives who "open doors" for you and in effect presell you to prospective clients.

The third element, *targets*, includes two types:

1. *Targets of Opportunity.* These include existing clients with needs, prospective clients in your pending new clients pipeline, desirable potential clients, and desirable market niches.

2. *Targets of Influence.*   These include other professionals who serve your clients, decision makers in prospective client organizations, executive directors of trade and professional associations, industry leaders, and others.

The fourth element, *promotion*, focuses on two broad areas:

1. *Personal Promotion.*   This area includes personal selling, joining and action letters.
2. *Nonpersonal Promotion.*   This area includes direct mail, publishing, advertising, and public relations.

Exhibit 1 illustrates the relationship of each element to the others.

EXHIBIT 1   CLIENT-CENTERED MARKETING MODEL

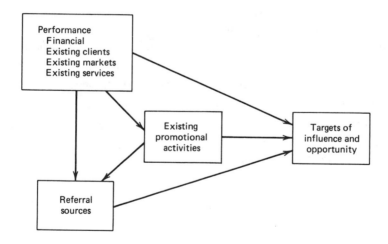

CLIENT-CENTERED SERVICES

Now let's develop a client-centered view of the services you provide. A professional service is largely an intangible idea that is purchased for the end results it will produce. As stated previously, clients don't really purchase services; they purchase the expectations of receiving a more favorable future. The future contains expected *benefits* to the purchaser.

A benefit is a perceived value satisfaction by the purchaser and is always related to the purchaser's needs and expectations about the way in which those needs and expectations will be met.

The worksheet that follows, the "client-centered service analysis," can be used to identify benefits that are important to clients and, indeed, to force you to think about services as your clients do.

To use the chart effectively, follow these steps:

1. Enter the name of the service you want to analyze on the top line.

2. Move to the upper left-hand block, "Improve or Enhance," and ask: "In what ways does this service enable purchasers or users to improve or enhance something they value?" List your answers in the block—for example, "improve market penetration," "enhance image," and so on.

3. Move next to the upper right-hand block and ask: "In what ways does this service reduce, relieve, or eliminate some unwanted condition?" List your answers in the block—for example, "reduce filing time," "relieve backlog pressures," and so forth.

4. Move to the "Protect" block and ask: "In what ways does this service enable the purchaser or users to protect something they value?" Again, list your answers in the block.

5. Then move to the remaining blocks and complete them in a similar manner.

Note: Not all blocks need to or will be completed for a given service.

You now have a set of potential benefits that can accrue to a client. The completed chart can be used in proposal writing and face-to-face discussions with clients and training staff.

A sample of how an accountant might complete the chart is presented in Exhibit 2a. The blank form is shown in Exhibit 2b.

Other key service words and phrases that could be used in filling out the client-centered service analysis are as follow:

Improve

Decision-making capability

Profits

Cash flow position

Internal operations

Public product image

Quality, reliability, effectiveness of software

Usefulness and relevance of documentation

Operating efficiency and productivity

Understanding of costs

Information for decisions

User service needs

Competitive capabilities

Employee morale and motivation

Employee safety

Market position

Enhance

Credibility of client's role in community

User orientation of software

Service to particular groups or users

Inherent advantages

For: <u>AUDIT SERVICES</u>

(Service)

Your task is to identify client needs and problem situations for which your service is appropriate. For each verb listed below, identify how your service applies. For example, under the word "eliminate" you might put "unnecessary forms and procedures."

Improve or Enhance	*Reduce, Relieve, or Eliminate*
Cash flow Profitability Accounting procedures Operations Revenues Internal control Internal reporting	Exposure to loss Paperwork Bottlenecks Investment debt Material errors Errors
Protect	*Restructure*
Assets Credibility Reputation Profit Lines of credit Liquidity	Quality of reporting system Unprofitable operations Unnecessary reports Branch operations
Develop or Install	*Restore or Resolve*

External reporting
Management information
   system
Cost systems
Decision-making model
	Image of client
	Reliability of financial
	   statements
	Resolve backlogs, uncertainty,
	   inefficiencies, management
	   anxiety

For: _____
                        (Service)

Your task is to identify client needs and problem situations for which your
service is appropriate. For each verb listed below, identify how your service
applies. For example, under the word "eliminate" you might put "unnecessary
forms and procedures."

Improve or Enhance	Reduce, Relieve, or Eliminate
Protect	Restructure
Identify	Restore or Resolve

Competitive edge

Utilization of equipment and facilities

Employee morale and motivation

Organizational image

Technical understanding of problem

Existing strengths and image

Status in peer group

Existing skills

Reduce

Number of internal and external conflicts

Costs

Deficits

Skills levels requirements

Service delays and unreliability

Excess capacity

Idle equipment time

Peaking of demands

Risk

Waste

Inefficiency

Relieve

Conflict

Congestion

Public pressure and adverse opinions

Recurring problems

Future cost pressures

Pressure and tension

Organization conflicts

Blockages to staff development

Undue workload

Eliminate

Inefficiencies and waste

Conflict

Constraints

Adverse criticism

Low cost–benefit ratios

Deficits

Pilferage and internal security problems

Unnecessary cost

Protect

Client reputation and integrity

Independence

Market position and market share

Security of product served

Proprietary information

Integrity and public image

Self-interests

Restructure

Organization

Current operations

Planning process

Compensation and incentive program

Internal operations

Technical approach

Marketing approach

Identify

Strategies

Key problem areas

Decision factors

Solutions to problem areas

Needs

Alternatives or options

Constraints or limits

Potentials

Restore and Revitalize

Role of organization in community

Profitable operations

Standardized development process

Deteriorating facilities and equipment

Markets, competitive edge, and profits

Management structure

Employee morale—motivation

Market penetration

Outdated skills

Cash flow

Your task is to identify specific needs situations and to relate and discuss relevant client benefits provided by your service.

In this chapter you have been exposed to the client-centered marketing model and the need for a client-centered orientation to marketing your services. The next several chapters will enable you to gain a sense of where you've been by assessing financial performance, present clients, and present markets.

3

ASSESSING FINANCIAL PERFORMANCE

THIS CHAPTER is short and sweet. Its sole purpose is to emphasize that benchmarks and indicators of previous performance are needed to enable you to move in a more prosperous direction— you have to know where you've been and where you're going.

A 3-year period is used to eliminate seasonal, cyclical, and unusual fluctuations in your personal practice such as providing an unusually large amount of special services to several of your largest clients.

A THREE-YEAR REVIEW

To complete this chapter you will need to obtain the following data for the latest 36 months (or if you've been in business for less than 36 months, for as long as you've been in practice):

The total fees you personally billed

The number of hours you personally invested in:
    Billable client work
    Marketing and practice development
    Other activities

Exhibit 3a can be used to list your *personal* billing performance. The blank form is listed in Exhibit 3b.

EXHIBIT 3a   THREE-YEAR FINANCIAL PERFORMANCE

Year	Revenue, $ U.S.	Growth, %
198_A	61,500	13.6
198_B	54,100	28.6
198_C	38,620	5.1 (over previous year, unlisted)

EXHIBIT 3b   THREE-YEAR FINANCIAL PERFORMANCE—BLANK FORM

Year	Revenue, $ U.S.	Growth, %
198__	_____	_____
198__	_____	_____
198__	_____	_____

PERFORMANCE TREND?

Does your 3-year performance profile suggest a trend or pattern? Does it meet your expectations?

If your situation indicates real growth, can you recruit and retain the staff you need? And are you:

1. Working harder and reaping more rewards?
2. Managing more and personally billing less?
3. Keeping pace with or outrunning other partners, practices, and inflation?

If your situation indicates a decline, are you surprised? Is it within tolerance limits? Are you aware of the reasons for the decline?

What can you conclude from this simple analysis? You may now wish to complete this analysis for other professionals in your firm (if applicable).

Exhibit 4a is used to list your hourly data. The blank form is listed in Exhibit 4b.

EXHIBIT 4a   THREE-YEAR DISTRIBUTION OF PERSONAL HOURS

Activity Areas	1983	1984	1985
Chargeable client work	1,408	1,877	1,806
Marketing and practice development	311	186	215
Other activities	602	440	383
Total	2,321	2,503	2,404

EXHIBIT 4b   THREE-YEAR DISTRIBUTION OF PERSONAL HOURS—BLANK FORM

Activity Areas	19___	19___	19___
Chargeable client work	_____	_____	_____
Marketing and practice development	_____	_____	_____
Other activities	_____	_____	_____
Total	======	======	======

Does your three-year profile suggest a trend or pattern? Does it meet your personal goals? You may find it useful to construct your own chart or spreadsheet to facilitate a more detailed financial analysis.

The important point is that you must establish benchmarks for billing rate, revenue growth, and distribution of personal hours to effectively critique previous performance and establish new, desirable performance goals.

In Chapter 4 we discuss how to assess or classify present clients— a very important and revealing exercise!

ASSESSING YOUR PRESENT CLIENTS

THIS CHAPTER focuses on the activities involved in identifying, classifying, and assessing the potential of your existing client base. On completion you should be able to answer these questions:

- ☐ How do "A," "B," "C," and "D" clients differ?
- ☐ Why must "A," "B," "C," and "D" clients be treated differently?
- ☐ Why is it harmful to give marginal clients "A" level of attention?

ALL CLIENTS ARE NOT EQUAL

Assessment of your present clients is a major step toward *capitalizing* on areas of opportunities. Your primary purpose is to identify your client–market–service mix as a basis for retaining and/or developing your desired mix for now and in the future. You may want to review this chapter often to ensure that you attain maximum comprehension of your present client base.

Leveraging your existing client base requires that you:

1. Classify your existing clients by estimating their potential for providing you with opportunities or problems by use of our suggested "A," "B," "C," and "D" approach.
2. Undertake appropriate actions with your "A" clients, your good "B" clients, marginal "C" clients, and troublesome "D" clients.
3. Identify and undertake corrective actions to remove causes of lost clients.
4. Undertake actions to capitalize on sources of desirable new clients (to be discussed in Chapter 7).

Exhibit 5 summarizes the characteristics of "A," "B," "C," and "D" clients and the activities that should be undertaken regarding each class.

CLASSIFICATION 101

First, classify your existing clients by your estimate of potential for providing you with opportunities or problems. Your purpose is to "take stock" of what you have to work with in your existing client base. You have a number of clients, each of whom has certain potential for providing you with opportunity or problems. Classification is essential because you (1) will have a baseline with which to measure your progress, (2) can concentrate your efforts on "A" clients with high potential, and (3) can better manage your client base.

Begin by assembling a list of your clients, and rank them in descending order by amount of fee produced during the most recent 12-month period (see Exhibit 6).

EXHIBIT 5   CLIENT CHARACTERISTICS

Client Type	Characteristics	Options
"A"	Realistic notion of situation Large fee size Willingly accepts large fee size Prestige client	Retention planning
	Contacts/referrals Ability to serve and satisfy Expanding needs of clients	Develop referrals
	Compatibility, "chemistry" Challenging work Enthusiastic about firm	Expand services
"B"	Pay willingly Annuity client	Upgrade to "A"
	Moderate to no growth Bread and butter	Serve as required
"C"	Fee and collection problems Temporary problem Educate the client and move to "B"	Upgrade to "B"
	Discuss fees/collections openly, and fairly	Tolerate
"D"	Difficult to impossible to work with Make you vulnerable "It's you who serves me or else!" Ask for unethical, unreasonable services	Terminate

27

EXHIBIT 6   TAKING STOCK OF EXISTING CLIENT BASE

Rank	Client	Service(s) Provided	Industry	Volume of Billing	Percentage
1					
2					
3					
4					
5					
6					
7					
8					

Now you are ready to classify each client using the "A," "B," "C," and "D" client characteristics in Exhibit 5. Remember, an "A" client is a *key* client. This type of client provides you with substantial revenue, may make referrals in your behalf, provide you with potential for additional services, and so forth.

Your "B" clients are your *fair-to-good* clients, who might be called your "bread-and-butter" clients. They pay their bills, make few demands, and seldom provide you with additional service opportunities.

Your "C" clients are your *marginal* clients who fit one of two categories: (1) they constitute fee problems because they represent excessive discount situations or are slow payers; or (2) they make you vulnerable or upset with their actions because they operate on the "edge" of ethical conduct or give you or your staff a hard time.

Your "D" clients must be dropped immediately. "D" clients routinely request you to compromise your standards or ethics. These are clients you wish you'd never met.

A firm installed a policy of reviewing and classifying all new clients after the first anniversary of service and of being more "up front" regarding its services delivery procedures during its new business discussions. The principals were taught to address prospects on the matter of fees by using a variation of the following statement:

> To produce the results we outlined, your budget for the project should
> be in the range of $_____ to $_____. Our practice is to invoice monthly
> as the work proceeds and payment is expected within *x* days of receipt.
> Do you see any difficulty with this arrangement?

Hopefully your "A" clients will account for a substantial portion of your revenue and provide you with growth opportunities. You will want to develop some additional information about them. Exhibit 7 is a convenient form for capturing important information.

List your clients' names first. Then, using the criteria listed in the upper right-hand portion of the worksheet, simply put an "X" in the appropriate column. For every key client with an "X" or brief one word description (i.e. "good") in the PS column, make a note in the "Remarks" column indicating possible expansion of services.

Now continue by listing any clients you feel may be developed into referrals. Hopefully you will have a substantial percentage of your clients in this category.

Your "B" clients pay their bills, are generally easy to work with, and can sometimes be developed into "A" clients. Be alert to identify needs and provide additional services as required. Exhibit 8 should be used to list any "B" clients that may have potential for upgrading.

Your "C" clients make their presence known quickly as they haggle over fees and occasionally want you to do something that you feel isn't right. Complete Exhibit 9, and look for patterns in those clients listed.

Don't waste any more time with "D" clients.

SERVE THE "A"s, DROP THE "D"s

Too often marginal clients receive "A" level attention, and, as a result, your present key clients may be neglected. Your three action steps are clear: (1) look for those few clients whom you can educate and influence to change and upgrade to a "B," (2) realistically identify those relatively few problem clients *you must* keep because of previous commitments, and (3) identify candidates for termination. For

EXHIBIT 7a EXISTING "A" CLIENTS

Client	Assessment					Fees			Estimated Next 12 Months		Remarks
	RS	PS	PT	QOR	Industry	Latest 12 Months	Percentage of Total, %		Hours	$	
XYZ Industries	Yellow Pages	Good	Good	4	Construction	$4,600	7.4		156	$5,000	All systems go
Jones Hardware	Advt.	—	Maybe	4	Hardware	1,260	2.0		142	4,400	Needs personal visit
EDP Systems Design Corp.	Bank	Excellent	Excellent	5	EDP	8,800	14.3		312	10,000	Superstar!
Hartmann Agency	Rotary	Maybe good	Maybe	5	Personnel	2,180	3.5		116	3,500	Keep in touch—Rotary
Systat, Inc.	Yellow Pages	?	?	3	EDP	5,800	7.4		48	1,500	Their move
The Conine Group	Yellow Pages	No	?	3	Executive Recruiters	2,250	3.6		—	—	Need new strategy
Mazur & Company	Neighbor	No	?	2	Executive Recruiters	2,750	4.4		—	—	Reclassify?
E. W. Woodson & Co.	EDP Systems	Good	Fair	4	Financial	2,230	3.6		113	3,600	OK
Mason Brothers	Reciprocal	Excellent	Excellent	4	Construction	3,110	5.1		250	8,000	Lunch! Now

Key: RS = referral source, PS = potential for additional services in short term—12 months, PT = potential for additional services in long term—beyond 12 months, QOR = quality of relationship (1 to 5) 1—poor, 5—perfect.

EXHIBIT 7b EXISTING "A" CLIENTS—BLANK FORM

Client	Assessment				Fees				Remarks
	RS	PS	PT	QOR	Industry	Latest 12 Months	Percentage of Total, %	Estimated Next 12 Months	
								Hours	$	

EXHIBIT 8a EXISTING "B" CLIENTS

| Client | Assessment | | | | Industry | Fees | | | | Remarks |
| | RS | PS | PT | QOR | | Latest 12 Months | Percentage of Total, % | Estimated Next 12 Months | | |
								Hours	$	
D. S. McGuire, Inc.	Yellow Pages	2	1	3	Contractors	$3,140	5.1	90	$2,900	Facing bankruptcy
Videomasters	Digitime	2	3	3	Video tape	2,400	3.9	85	2,700	Can't move them
Henson Janitorial	Digitime	1	?	2	Janitorial	980	1.6	10	300	
Digitime, Inc.	Read about us	3	4	5	Appliances	3,170	5.2	200	6,400	Ready for "A" status?
R. Hayes & Assoc.	College friend	3	3	4	Advertising Agency	1,010	1.6	115	3,700	
Rossini Bros. Pizza	Friend	2	2	5	Restaurant	280	0.4	50?	1,600	?
Amer. Assoc. of Travel	Delta Travel	—	2	2	Association	4,250	6.9	—	—	Unhappy, need to call
Sunrise Society	Wife's friend	2	2	4	Condo development	3,740	6.1	80	2,500	Lost our touch

Key: **RS** = referral source, **PS** = potential for additional services in short term—12 months, **PT** = potential for additional services in long term—beyond 12 months, **QOR** = quality of relationship (1 to 5) 1—poor, 5—perfect.

EXHIBIT 8b EXISTING "B" CLIENTS—BLANK FORM

Client	Assessment				Fees					Remarks
	RS	PS	PT	QOR	Industry	Latest 12 Months	Percentage of Total, %	Estimated Next 12 Months		
								Hours	$	

EXHIBIT 9a EXISTING "C" AND "D" CLIENTS

Client	Type "C"[a]	Type "D"[b]	Fees Latest 12 Months	Fees Percentage of Total, %	Fees Estimated Next 12 Months	Industry	Remarks
Exeter Systems	✓		$ 180	0.3	$ 240	Energy management consultants	Nickel and dimer
Mgmt. Resources Unlimited	✓		1,800	3.0	1,400		Wants too much
Ernest Greenwood		✓	110	0.2	—	Landscape	Get fee and drop!
Studio Portraits Prof.	✓		290	0.5	—	Photo.	?
The Lamp Group	✓		260	0.4	520	Career Planning	Needs pep talk
New Age Foods		✓	650	1.0	250	Food	Get money and drop if no improvement
S. Western Auto Supply		✓	800	1.3	800	Distribution Auto parts	Wait and see
Garden Grove		✓	350	0.7	—	Nursery	Out of business
Luna's	✓		580	0.9	580	Cafe	Same as last year
The Paper Tree	✓		180	0.2	360	Office Supply	O.K.
Ogden's	✓		960	1.6	600	Restaurant	Screwy management
Sword & Scissor		✓	1,450	2.3	900	Cutlery	Difficult!
Myers & Fuchs Realty	✓		570	0.9	140	Realtors	No new needs
Hair-Well	✓		1,370	2.2	2,000	Salon	Move to "B"
			$9,550 total		$7,790 total		

[a]Excessive discount or collection problem.

[b]Problem with personnel, reputation, and so on.

EXHIBIT 9b EXISTING "C" AND "D" CLIENTS—BLANK FORM

Client	Type		Fees			Industry	Remarks
	"C"	"D"	Latest 12 Months	Percentage of Total, %	Estimated Next 12 Months		
			$_____ total		$_____ total		

every five "D" (or possibly "C") hours terminated, you'll gain 10 hours more energy and enjoyment.

A "D" client is often created when the professional "caves in" on a matter of policy. During a seminar conducted for a group of managing partners of actuarial firms, we examined the anatomy of a "D" client and realized that such a client is often educated to behave in this manner.

One possible solution to "D" clients involves analysis of the cause(s) of this particular client situation. The professional should accept responsibility for the situation and reeducate the client, pointing out that conditions have changed. The relationship must then be renegotiated.

ASSESSMENT PAYS OFF

If you're like most professionals, you have probably never assessed and listed your clients in the manner described in this chapter. Yet, after doing so, you'll readily see that assessment of the present client base is essential for understanding the nature of your practice and for beginning to develop a framework for attracting more "A" and "B" clients.

In Chapter 5 we focus on your primary markets using a similar assessment technique.

ASSESSING YOUR PRIMARY AND POTENTIAL MARKET(S)

THE PURPOSE of this chapter is to expand your horizons in the assessment of present and potential market areas. The information and exercises that follow provide you with the "tools" to broaden and strengthen your client base and will enable you to answer these questions:

☐ What is a primary market? What is your primary market?

☐ What human sources can provide information about new markets?

☐ What printed sources of information will enable you to learn about new markets?

☐ How can I inexpensively research new potential markets?

WHAT IS YOUR MARKET?

Your existing markets, groups of clients within similar industries, make up the "arenas" in which you practice and prosper. A market consists of all actual and potential clients and those individuals who are influential in using, retaining, and referring you and your services. Becoming aware of your primary markets enables you to:

1. Find a niche or segment in which you enjoy serving and produce exceptional results so that you can attempt to "dominate" it.
2. Identify high-potential areas for concentration and leveraging.
3. Abandon or cut back in markets that may be "drying up" or attracting too much competition.

A primary market is one that constitutes a relatively large percentage of your total revenue. Ideally, you should have several primary markets with countercyclical performance patterns providing a relatively stable assignment load.

Use the blank chart in Exhibit 10*b* to compare the percent of total fees you earn by industry. A sample completed chart is presented in Exhibit 10*a*.

A HARD LOOK AT THE MARKETS

Refer to your list of markets and estimate the potential for growth both in the short term, within 12 months; and long term, beyond 12 months. Assign values from one (1) for no growth up to five (5), which suggest certain and substantial growth.

Thoughtfully consider and answer the question: "Are these primary markets the ones I should or want to be in?" If not, determine any secondary markets that warrant your attention for analysis, planning, and action, for these may become your primary markets.

After attending a marketing seminar for professional services, a professional "profiled" her practice by determining the percentage of

EXHIBIT 10a CURRENT PRIMARY AND SECONDARY MARKETS

Market	Percentage of Revenue, %	Description of Market	Potential for Growth Short Term	Long Term
		Current Primary Markets		
1. Professional Services	24.9	Emerging firms, good base	5[a]	5
2. EDP	23.8	Small firms, questionable	4	3
3. Construction	17.8	Not high interest, market good	3	3
4. Retailing	17.1	Getting stronger	4	5
5.				
6.				
7.				
8.				
		Current Secondary Markets		
1. Associations	9.1	Good market, experience limited	3	5
2. Realty (subset of #1 above)	7.0	Fluctuates with economy	3	4
3. Telecommunications	?	Excellent growth	2	5?
4.				
5.				
6.				
7.				
8.				

[a]5 = best.

EXHIBIT 10*b*   CURRENT PRIMARY AND SECONDARY MARKETS—
BLANK FORM

Market	Percentage of Revenue, %	Description of Market	Potential for Growth	
			Short Term	Long Term

Current Primary Markets

1. _____ _____ _____ _____
2. _____ _____ _____ _____
3. _____ _____ _____ _____
4. _____ _____ _____ _____
5. _____ _____ _____ _____
6. _____ _____ _____ _____
7. _____ _____ _____ _____
8. _____ _____ _____ _____

Current Secondary Markets

1. _____ _____ _____ _____
2. _____ _____ _____ _____
3. _____ _____ _____ _____
4. _____ _____ _____ _____
5. _____ _____ _____ _____
6. _____ _____ _____ _____
7. _____ _____ _____ _____
8. _____ _____ _____ _____

total and projected fees for each of her primary markets. Then she used the various research documents available to target industries to estimate the potential for industry growth and for growth of her types of service. She did this by talking with other suppliers of business and professional services. After telephoning directors of several associations comprised of member firms who were both clients and targets, she confirmed her suspicion that she had indeed selected a "rich niche" for study, analysis, and concentration.

WHAT ABOUT OTHER MARKETS?

In examining other markets, inexpensively, you may wish to consult your key clients, industry associates, studies, analysts, and stockbrokers. You may wish to review corporate and industry directories such as *Standard & Poor's, Moody's,* or *Dun & Bradstreet.*

Your public library maintains a copy of the *Business Periodicals Index,* the *Readers' Guide to Periodical Literature,* and the *Reader's Guide to Scientific Literature.* You may scan these indices for the latest articles in selected industry areas. For example, using the *Business Periodicals Index,* you can obtain the listing of all the articles in the last month, quarter, year, or 50 years, appearing in such nationally known business journals as *Business Week, Fortune, Forbes,* and *The Harvard Business Review,* as well as numerous other business periodicals.

Your public library also maintains a generous supply of telephone directories for both your geographic area and major cities across the United States. These serve as good starting points for identifying clients.

Association directories can be found in any library and offer the names, addresses, and telephone numbers of industry, trade, and professional associations. Three directories in particular—*Gales Directory of Associations, Ayers Association Directory,* and *National Trade and Professional Associations*—collectively offer over 6,000 association listings. The associations themselves can provide industry trend information, surveys, publications, and many other services.

An advertising agency in Tulsa, Oklahoma was able to identify hundreds of medium-size retailers in their local area by obtaining a directory published by a state retail trade association.

If you would like to research information that appeared in your local newspaper, consult your public library, which will usually contain a newspaper index that abstracts newspaper articles by topic and cross references this listing by date. The *Wall Street Journal Index*, for example, is available in many public libraries in major cities.

If you wish to identify a specific or perhaps obscure industry or trade journal, consult *Working Press of the Nation*, *Writer's Market*, *Bacon's Publicity Checker*, or the *Standard Periodicals Directory*. These directories are updated annually and collectively contain listings of over 10,000 technical and trade publications. By purchasing the subscription list of *Engineering News Record*, a graphic design firm in Minneapolis obtained dozens of new business leads through an effective direct mail campaign.

Suppliers' guides, often called *blue books* or *red books*, can be found in the business reference section of many public libraries. For example, the *Blue Book of Metro Area Home Builders* and *Red Book of Plumbing Supply Contractors** might be distributed by the local associations serving these industries.

Thomas' Register and *Cahners Buyer's Guide* contain a wealth of information on durable goods suppliers and can be used as target market lists.

FEDERAL GOVERNMENT INFORMATION SOURCES

The federal government is one of the largest publishers in the world. Through the Bureau of Census of the Department of Commerce, you may obtain sales and revenue data on virtually any industry by state, county, and standard metropolitan statistical area. Although the Bureau of Census is known primarily for its population reports, a census of business is taken on the second and seventh year of each

*These are theoretical, not actual, titles.

decade and is generally available 18 to 24 months thereafter. The Bureau of Census also produces many special industry reports and offers several ways to access their files. To obtain a list of the bureau's publications, write to:

Public Information Office
Bureau of the Census
Department of Commerce
Washington, DC 20233
(301) 763-4051

The Department of Commerce also produces the *U.S. Industrial Outlook*, which traces the growth of 200 industries and provides five-year forecasts for each industry. The *U.S. Statistical Abstract* is a compilation of data and reports from the Department of Commerce, the Department of Labor, the Department of Transportation, the Small Business Administration, and other federal agencies. The *Statistical Abstract* is particularly useful because it contains over 800 charts and graphs.

If you need to access information within a specific federal government agency, it is best to call the Public Information Office rather than the agency switchboard. When trying to identify a specific individual, ask for the Locator's Office, and when trying to identify a specific nonclassified document, use the Freedom of Information Office. Many of the telephone numbers you will need when asking the federal government for information are listed in Exhibits 11 and 12.

Many of the major publications produced by the federal government are on sale at the U.S. Government Printing Office. For a free catalogue, write to:

Superintendent of Documents
U.S. Government Printing Office
Washington, DC 20401

The federally sponsored National Technical Information Service (NTIS) maintains abstracts and data bases in 28 technical areas, such as engineering and energy. Descriptive brochures may be obtained by writing to:

EXHIBIT 11   FEDERAL INFORMATION CENTERS

Alabama			*Louisiana*	
Birmingham	205-322-8591		New Orleans	504-589-6696
Mobile	205-438-1421		*Maryland*	
Alaska			Baltimore	301-962-4980
Anchorage	907-271-3650		*Massachusetts*	
Arizona			Boston	617-223-7121
Phoenix	602-261-3313		*Michigan*	
Arkansas			Detroit	313-226-7016
Little Rock	501-378-6177		Grand Rapids	616-451-2628
California			*Minnesota*	
Los Angeles	213-688-3800		Minneapolis	612-349-5333
Sacramento	916-440-3344		*Missouri*	
San Diego	19-293-6030		St. Louis	314-425-4106
San Francisco	415-556-6600		Other towns	800-392-7711
Santa Ana	714-836-2386		*Nebraska*	
Colorado			Omaha	402-221-3353
Colorado Springs	303-471-9491		Other towns	800-642-8383
Denver	303-234-7181		*New Jersey*	
Pueblo	303-544-9523		Newark	201-645-3600
Connecticut			Trenton	609-396-4400
Hartford	203-527-2617		*New Mexico*	
New Haven	203-624-4720		Albuquerque	505-766-3091
Florida			*New York*	
St. Petersburg	813½893-3495		Albany	518-463-4421
Tampa	813-229-7911		Buffalo	716-846-4010
Other towns	800-282-8556		New York	212-264-4464
Georgia			Rochester	716-546-5075
Atlanta	404-221-6891		Syracuse	315-476-8545
Hawaii			*North Carolina*	
Honolulu	808-546-8620		Charlotte	704-376-3600
Illinois			*Ohio*	
Chicago	312-353-4242		Akron	216-375-5638
Indiana			Cincinnati	513-684-2801
Gary	219-883-4110		Cleveland	216-522-4040
Indianapolis	317-269-7373		Columbus	614-221-1014
Iowa	800-532-1556		Dayton	513-223-7377
Kansas	800-432-2934		Toledo	419-241-3223
Kentucky			*Oklahoma*	
Louisville	02-589-6261		Oklahoma City	405-231-4868
			Tulsa	918-584-4193

EXHIBIT 11 (continued)

Oregon		Fort Worth	817-334-3624
Portland	503-221-2222	Houston	713-229-2552
Pennsylvania		San Antonio	512-224-4471
Philadelphia	215-597-7042	Utah	
Pittsburgh	412-644-3456	Salt Lake City	801-524-5353
Rhode Island		Virginia	
Providence	401-331-5565	Norfolk	804-441-3101
Tennessee		Richmond	804-645-4928
Chattanooga	615-265-8231	Roanoke	703-982-8591
Memphis	901-521-3285	Washington	
Nashville	615-242-5056	Seattle	206-442-0570
Texas		Tacoma	206-383-5230
Austin	512-472-5494	Wisconsin	
Dallas	214-767-8585	Milwaukee	414-271-2273

EXHIBIT 12 FEDERAL AGENCY PUBLIC INFORMATION OFFICE TELEPHONE NUMBERS[a]

Agriculture	447-2791	Interstate Commerce	
Commerce	377-3263	Commission	375-7252
Defense	697-5131	National Aeronautics and	
Air Force	697-6061	Space Administration	755-3828
Army	697-7589	National Labor Relations	
Navy	697-7391	Board	632-4950
Education	245-8601	National Science	
Energy	252-6827	Foundation	357-9498
Health and Human Services	245-1850	Occupational Safety and Health	
Housing and Urban		Review Commission	634-7943
Development	755-6980	Office of Personnel	
Interior	343-3171	Management	632-5491
Labor	523-7316	Overseas Private Investment	
State	632-6575	Corporation	653-2800
Transportation	426-4570	Securities and Exchange	
Environmental Protection		Commission	272-2650
Agency	382-4355	Small Business	
Farm Credit Administration	755-2170	Administration	653-6822
Federal Communications		United States International	
Commission	254-7674	Trade Commission	523-0235
Federal Trade Commission	523-3830	United States Postal Service	245-4144
General Services		Veterans Administration	389-2443
Administration	523-1250		

[a]All numbers are preceded by area code 202.

National Technical Information Service
Department of Commerce
5285 Port Royal Road
Springfield, VA 22161
(703) 487-4600

Remember that, as a taxpayer, you have already paid for many of the federal government information sources that have been established. Use them!

STATE GOVERNMENT INFORMATION SOURCES

Nearly all of the 50 states have their own Department of Commerce, many have their own Department of Energy, and a few have special small business offices. The state capital, the state capital library, the governor's office, and the offices of your elected representatives often maintain special reports, studies, and analyses that may prove useful in your research efforts.

On a regional or local basis, various planning committees, the Chamber of Commerce, the research department of newspapers, highway commissions, local libraries, and the county courthouse are just a few of the information sources you may wish to tap. Many professionals have found that a wealth of information can be gained over the telephone or by simply visiting nearby organizations or agencies.

PUBLISHERS

Several key publishers, including Gale Press, Book Tower, Detroit, MI 48226; Facts on File, 460 Park Avenue South, New York, NY 10016; and John Wiley & Sons, 605 Third Avenue, New York, NY 10158 offer free catalogs listing numerous information directories that they publish. The Gale Press, for example, offers a directory of consultants and consulting organizations, a guide to research centers, and even a directory of directories.

NEWSLETTERS

Newsletters have become a valuable source of research information. Newsletters are now published by all industry groups and major associations. The *Oxbridge Newsletter Directory* lists several thousand newsletters, arranged by functional area. *National Trade and Professional Associations* indicates which, of the thousands of associations listed, maintain a newsletter. By accessing these directories and others suggested by your local librarian, you can gain access to valuable, inside information related to new primary markets. Many newsletters are read religiously by their subscribers. If you read what your target market reads, then you can more readily serve that market.

The ability to effectively gather valuable information is directly related to how organized you are. It may be necessary to befriend information sources such as librarians, publishers, and federal agency representatives because you will often have the need to call on these people more than once.

The assessment technique and research methodologies discussed in this chapter have been specifically geared to the professional who does not have the resources to undertake exhaustive research efforts. Once you or your staff have become familiar with the reference sources cited, the task of generating timely effective research information will become easier.

6

LEVERAGING YOUR CLIENTS

$\equiv$

THIS CHAPTER focuses on getting the greatest marketing return from effective interaction with your present clients through leveraging. Leveraging your clients encompasses various activities, including expanding client services and improving or salvaging relationships. Questions that you should be able to answer include:

☐   How can services to existing clients be expanded?

☐   What is client retention planning? When is it required?

☐   What are some basic causes of losing clients? What corrective action can be taken?

THAR'S GOLD IN THEM HILLS!

Leveraging your present clients is like mining the gold in your own backyard. You probably have existing and previous receptive clients with additional needs. In serving this target group there are three activities you can take:

1. Respond effectively to inquiries made by client executives. A number of unexpected inquiries may indicate a lack of client-centered attention.
2. Maintain communications with key client personnel during and between engagements.
3. Make self-initiated new business contacts to discuss needs and possible solutions.

When seeking to expand service, remember that your existing key clients are valuable resources that need to be cultivated. They provide you with a virtual "captive" market since you have already earned the right to discuss need situations with them.

Many service firms tend to place a premium on highly visible new clients and promotional activities and, as a result, may discourage staff and more reticent partners from participating in the marketing program. The solution is to recognize less visible, more intrinsic activities involved in retaining clients, expanding services to existing clients, and developing referrals.

Your goal is not to sell additional services, but to assist clients in achieving objectives through the appropriate use of your resources. Your role should be a conduit to the resources available within your firm.

Here are some action ideas:

1. Develop and expand your client-centered data bank and identify needs and problems.
2. Match priority client needs with capabilities and personalities of staff serving client, and bring priority needs to the attention of appropriate client personnel.
3. Use management letters and telephone calls to identify needs, plant "seeds of need" with client personnel, obtain new data and

verify the needs identified, and develop more involved relationships.

4. Improve communications and working relationships both during and between the service engagements to demonstrate interest.

A firm adopted the idea of "planting a seed of need" with clients judged to have additional needs in which they could be induced to invest. During the course of the engagement experienced staff would plant the seed of need by pinpointing industry performance benchmarks that were being met.

STRENGTHENING THE TIES

Leveraging your clients also involves improving or salvaging relationships with some of them. Understandably, effort will be required with some of your clients simply to retain them. The task of attracting and creating new clients and retaining your better clients should receive equal attention. When you assessed your clients (back in Chapter 4) some of the relationships rated a "3" or less out of five. A low-quality rating suggests the need for client retention planning.

Your existing clients are an essential resource that must be protected. Your best clients are probably targeted for attention by other aggressive firms. Then, too, changes in personnel can also lead to a decision to replace your firm or to establish relationships with other professionals. There are several indicators of client unrest, including:

Aggressive efforts on the part of competition.

Client complaints.

Unusual silence or indifference.

The best way to remedy a diminishing relationship is to document and assess the client–firm relationship, paying particular attention to these items:

History	People
Services	Pluses
Fees	Minuses

QUALITY OF RELATIONSHIP

Assess the nature and quality of existing relationships and identify any problems to be handled. Often a plan must be devised to improve your working relationship with a client. This may necessitate upgrading your "visibility of value," that is, informing your clients of everything you're doing for them and how they can apply your services for greatest return. Good or improved communication, of course, is part and parcel to any successful professional service engagement.

A rule of thumb relative to clients is that when *you* think there is a problem, there most assuredly is.

Identify and undertake corrective action to remove causes of lost clients. Recognizing the sources of desirable new clients and the reasons for losing good clients during the most recent three years illustrates the effectiveness of the firm's present marketing efforts. Accurate and timely information for each source and reason is needed. You may choose to develop or modify new clientele and client termination forms and reporting procedures to generate these data.

This analysis, if performed on a quarterly basis, will illustrate the results of the firm's marketing activity and identify opportunities and problems that need to be handled.

ADDING UP THE SCORE

The chart shown in Exhibit 13 can be used to identify the causes of lost clients and thus reveal a picture of the "health" of your practice. Review this carefully, and list any steps you can take to reduce the number of clients lost.

EXHIBIT 13a CLIENTS ACQUIRED/LOST SUMMARY

Start date			Present date		
Clients Acquired			Clients Lost		
Source	Number	Fees	Reasons	Number	Fees
Client referrals	10	$ 24,800	Fee complaint	2	$ 2,460
Leads from recommendations		$	Service complaint	3	$ 1,110
Drop-ins/image	3	$ 5,550	Moved out of market	1	$ 280
Targeted, self-initiated action	6	$ 11,310	Merger or acquisition	1	$ 950
Advertising	9	$ 19,050	Bankruptcy	1	$ 350
Unknown	3	$ 790	Outside pressure Bank	1	$ 800
			Government		$
			Sale of business		$
			Unknown	2	$ 1,340

EXHIBIT 13b CLIENTS ACQUIRED/LOST SUMMARY— BLANK FORM

Start date			Present date		
Clients Acquired			Clients Lost		
Source	Number	Fees	Reasons	Number	Fees
Client referrals		$	Fee complaint		$
Leads from recommendations		$	Service complaint		$
Drop-ins/image		$	Moved out of market		$
Targeted, self-initiated action		$	Merger or acquisition		$
Advertising		$	Bankruptcy		$
Unknown		$	Outside pressure Bank		$
			Government		$
			Sale of business		$
			Unknown		$

This chapter probably asked you to examine your client base in a new way. The need for leveraging of the existing client base should now be clear.

By developing a client-centered marketing orientation and using leveraging, you can achieve optimum return for your marketing efforts. Next, let's look at the all-important process of cultivating referrals.

CULTIVATING REFERRALS

CULTIVATING REFERRALS is the backbone of a successful practice. Yet, too many professionals regard this as a burdensome, or worse, unimportant task. This chapter discusses identification, education, and leveraging of your relationships with those clients and nonclients who make referrals and introductions and provide you with leads. This chapter provides the answers to these questions:

- [ ] Why are good referrals important?
- [ ] What are the two classes of referral source?
- [ ] What is the best way to show appreciation for the efforts made by referral sources?
- [ ] What are six possible nonclient referral sources?
- [ ] How does the development of a master list of client referral sources and targets of influence aid analysis, planning, and action?

WORKING EASIER

Good referrals make your marketing task easier and your work more interesting, profitable, and satisfying. Development of referrals cannot be left to chance. Think of referrals as 24-hour, unpaid sales representatives who are promoting you and your firm.

TWO CLASSES OF REFERRAL

There are two classes of referral:

1. Satisfied or enthusiastic existing and previous clients who have referred other potential clients to you or enabled you to participate in their industry activities.
2. Existing nonclient influentials such as attorneys and bankers who have provided you with leads or mentioned you to their clients and others.

Identification of your client referral sources is a revealing and highly useful exercise.

One experienced professional created referrals by managing a three-step process: (1) defining the client's objectives; (2) planning the client's projects for early, visible results; and (3) conducting end-of-engagement "satisfaction" meetings.

Use the chart given in Exhibit 14 to list the names of clients and previous clients who have made referrals in your behalf. If convenient, refer back to Exhibit 7.

RATING YOUR REFERRAL SOURCES

Now list the names, titles, and organization affiliation of those who have made referrals for you. Also estimate the quality of relationship (1 to 5) as you did with your key clients and then complete the chart

EXHIBIT 14a   CLIENT REFERRAL SOURCES

Name, Title, and Organization	Quality of Relationship (1 to 5)	What Sources of New Business Does (S)He Represent?	How Do I Plan to Use this Referral Source?
William Reeves, 1st State Bank	5	EDP Systems Design	Mention success with EDP Systems Design
Wilford Harrison (Rotary)	4	Hartmann Agency	Mention Hartmann's expansion
Louise McDaniels—neighbor	3	Mazur & Co.	?
EDP Systems Design Corp.	5	E.W. Woodward & Co and Management Resources Unlimited	EDP—turn into showcase client
Digitime	5	Videomasters	Change to "A" status, send note
Eddy Scarlata	5	Robert Hayes Assoc.	Ask Eddy for others
Delta Travel	2	ARTA	Trouble—rethink this one
Ed Turner	4	Sunrise Society	Get referral for Turner
James Gibson	2	New Age Foods	Invite to March 8 reception
Wilson S. Brown, Attorney	3	Luna's	Lunch!
Automak	3	Ogden's	Educate regarding other capabilities

Note: 5 = Best.

57

EXHIBIT 14b CLIENT REFERRAL SOURCES—BLANK FORM

Name, Title, and Organization	Quality of Relationship (1 to 5)	What Sources of New Business Does (S)He Represent?	How Do I Plan to Use this Referral Source?

by answering and listing your answers to the two questions in the columns on the chart.

Organizations, firms, and individuals that may have need for your services can be called *targets of opportunity* because they literally represent service and revenue opportunities for your firm. Both existing clients and nonclients may assist you in identifying and contacting targets of opportunity.

When analyzing your referral sources, consider:

1. How many referral sources do I have in my primary markets?
2. Why are these clients making referrals? Why aren't other good clients making referrals in my behalf?
3. What is the quality of my relationship with my key referral sources? As a general rule, a score of 3 or less means you need to enhance the relationship.
4. How frequently do I contact these referral sources to thank them for their efforts and seek additional referrals?

TARGETS OF INFLUENCE: IDENTIFYING YOUR NONCLIENT INFLUENTIALS

Strategic decisions and actions to be undertaken to effectively maintain and further broaden your preferred client service market mix and referral sources are discussed in this section. We have termed nonclient referral sources as *targets of influence*.

Exhibit 15 should be used as a guide to list the names of your nonclient influentials, such as:

Accountants	Attorneys
Politicians	Editors
Alumni of your firm	Board members
Bankers and investment bankers	Peers
Association executives	Industry leaders
Insurance agents	Other influentials

EXHIBIT 15a   TARGETS OF INFLUENCE

Names and Affiliations of Influential Contacts	QOR (1 to 5)	How Do I Plan to Effectively Use My Relationship with These People?
Donald Bower, VP State Bank	5	Seek introduction to Howard Lumber Co.
Thomas Hague, City Councilman	4	—
Helen Seghers, Editor—Panorama	5	Submit article
Nancy Fresin, Administration— Reston Soc.	5	Get invited to next meeting
Ralph Delman, Attorney at Law	3	Volunteer on campaign
Russell E. Haspel, 1st Federal	3	Send Thanks
Albert Foley, Insurance	5	Exchange referrals
Tom Stratton, Editor— Evening Star	4	Send news release
Agnes Holmes, Director ADLA	3	Seek board nomination
Herb Seltzer, Insurance	5	Get introduction to M. Sanders
Morrie Landstrom, SBA Management Asst.	3	Join A.C.E.

EXHIBIT 15b   TARGETS OF INFLUENCE—BLANK FORM

Names and Affiliations of Influential Contacts	QOR (1 to 5)	How Do I Plan to Effectively Use My Relationship with These People?

THANK YOU, THANK YOU

After you have identified all client and nonclient referral sources, your next mission is to acknowledge your referral sources' assistance to you and to "educate" them about the kind of new client(s) and/or market(s) you are best able to serve. Ask referral sources for introductions to industry and/or market opinion leaders and so on. People generally like to assist others who have a sense of purpose and gratitude.

In reviewing your list of nonclient referral sources, ask yourself:

1. How many influential relationships, such as attorneys and bankers, do I have in each category?
2. What makes these particular individuals influential? Why do they provide me with leads?
3. What is the quality of my relationship with key influential associates?
4. How frequently do I contact these influentials to thank them for their efforts and seek additional leads?
5. How frequently do I reciprocate by making appropriate referrals to them?

After answering these questions, many professionals find that they have been lax in the cultivation and maintenance of referrals.

For years a top partner in a law firm had obtained leads from the lending officer in a prestigious bank. He became complacent, however, and admittedly took the referral source for granted—he lengthened the time between contacts and increasingly neglected to send follow-up thank you notes or to provide feedback to the lending officer. One day the partner realized that this once fertile referral source had dried up. To this day, he has been unable to turn the flow of leads back on.

If you find yourself in the lax category, why not resolve now to begin an aggressive campaign to develop and cultivate referral sources?

KFEPING TRACK ON NEW LEADS

You may have some use for one additional chart, that given in
Exhibit 16. As your referral program begins to pay off, new leads can
be entered here.

EXHIBIT 16   DESIRABLE POTENTIAL CLIENTS

Potential Client	Service Opportunities	Plan for Conversion to Paying Client
		(Cont.)

The management of an EDP consulting firm on the West Coast
capitalized on the high level of "job hopping" that was evident in the
industry they served. Second- and third-level professional staff were
given responsibility for developing relationships with acknowledged
"fast trackers" or "up and comers."

Each professional was responsible for developing and maintaining the relationship and being alert to situations where employees left
their present jobs for greener pastures. A follow-up phone call and
letter wishing the person well in their position coupled with periodic
contacts led to the establishment of sound relationships in nonclient
organizations.

Such relationships, when carefully nurtured, provide a relatively
comfortable new business approach.

This chapter has focused on the importance of identifying and
capitalizing on client and nonclient referral sources. Chapter 8 discusses another source for identifying new business: effective prospecting techniques.

8

PROSPECTING LIKE
A "PRO"

PROSPECTING IS the task of securing appointments with "qualified" nonclients and is an important component in the overall client-centered marketing effort. Mastery of effective prospecting techniques enables you to maximize your available time allocated to marketing. In this chapter we review effective prospecting techniques and provide the answers to these questions:

☐ Why is "homework" an essential component of prospecting?

☐ Why is the client-centered marketing approach crucial to effective prospecting?

GET CRACKIN'

Waiting for the phone to ring or for clients or prospects to contact you rarely leads to successful marketing results. Getting on the phone and making things happen are the early links in the chain that lead to profitable sales success.

Before attempting to generate or "work" a prospect list, it's important to profile or define the market you're attempting to penetrate and why your services meet the needs of this market. Many professionals fluctuate from day to day or week to week, continuously making halfhearted efforts to penetrate first one market, then a second, then back to the first, and then a third. They never stop to carefully analyze which market they should penetrate first. (If needed, refer back to information presented in Chapter 5 on researching new markets.)

The best way to solve this problem is to use the client-centered approach. First, identify the needs and then devise strategies to serve those needs (better than your competition can). A common mistake that all of us make is to get overinvolved in the services that we provide and forget to align our thinking in terms of what the identified target market needs. One way to determine whether your services are appropriate for a chosen target market is to learn about the experience that other professionals within your industry have had in serving this market. Another factor to consider is what developments have occurred in the political, economic, technological, business, and social environments that have resulted in new needs on the part of target markets and to match your capabilities to the needs.

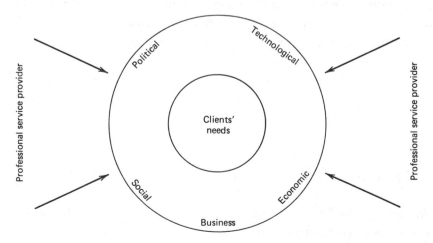

DEVELOPING AND PROPERLY WORKING YOUR PROSPECT LIST

There are several ways of developing a prospect list. Literature scans, use of industry directories, analyses of financial and operating ratios, business periodicals literature scans, purchase of industry reports, and use of consultants and attendance at specialized seminars are appropriate techniques for the busy professional.

Working your prospect list involves calling all parties using spaced intervals between completion of calls and start of next call. It also means calling everyone on the entire list and not letting the result of the first few calls dampen your original enthusiasm. Many professionals become discouraged because of rejection after a relatively short time. The winners, however, realize that successful prospecting means paying homage to the numbers game. Every "No" brings you closer to a "Yes."

DO YOUR HOMEWORK

A second important step in effective prospecting is to learn about the operating characteristics of the industry or businesses—or individuals —to whom you wish to sell.

1. What in your past experience can be drawn on and used as a competitive advantage in penetrating your chosen market?
2. How have your services traditionally been accepted and used by the target market? What can you presently offer that is consistent with the changing needs of the target market?

"Homework" is often a dreaded component of effective prospecting. Yet, if you lack a minimum amount of reliable, up-to-date information about your target market, any attempts at penetrating the market will either fall completely flat or will be shaky for the first few calls as you scramble to rework your presentation, using terminology and citing examples to which prospects can relate.

Properly working the list also requires careful monitoring and tracking of each phone call denoting who should be called back and when, who wasn't in, who'll be returning your call, who's moved or has a number that is no longer working, and so forth. Any organized spreadsheet, chart, or notebook will do when tracking progress through prospecting. Later you can transfer the most promising prospects to the chart given in Exhibit 16.

A common mistake is to begin working the list, not keep careful records, be called away on business, and then attempt to begin working on the list again. The problems encountered, such as wondering if you already called someone, will utterly destroy your self-confidence when you make additional calls, for fear of embarrassment. The fastest way to ruin a perfectly good prospect list is to not keep a careful log of all correspondence. The way to use the prospect list to fullest advantage is to maintain an accurate, up-to-date log. It's as simple as that.

WORK A CURRENT LIST

An all-too-common problem is to rely on a list that may contain faulty information, has aged considerably, or for any number of other reasons is an inferior list. Though the temptation may be great, use only lists that you've generated yourself or, at least, had a hand in identifying or creating. It's discouraging to begin making calls only to realize that the individual named has since moved or departed from a particular company or does not have the authority you are seeking.

OVERRELIANCE ON TRADITIONAL SOURCES

Harold Gray, a principal with a professional service firm in a metropolitan area, had developed a knack for identifying appropriate target markets and developing prospect lists to penetrate those markets.

He frequently talked with Stuart Rogers, a new partner, who had not been selling well. When Harold asked Stuart what he knew about the XYZ Industry, Stuart's reply was, "Oh, I don't think it's doing so well right now. I'd forget that one if I were you." Luckily, Harold did not overrely on traditional information sources—in this case a colleague —in determining the level of effort he would make in penetrating this particular market.

Harold bolstered his knowledge by talking to professionals in other fields, by doing some simple library research and by reading a Department of Commerce report on the industry. He soon learned that although the industry had had several slow quarters of late, in the last six months industry sales had rebounded well. On the basis of this information, Harold decided that now would be a good time to penetrate this market and use his prospect list.

PREPARE A TIME AND MONEY BUDGET

Effective prospecting necessitates the allocation of sufficient time to work the prospect list, make sales calls, make follow-ups, and close *and* a sufficient budget in support of the sales effort. Another common mistake is to underestimate the time necessary to successfully penetrate a market and to attempt to overeconomize in support of the selling effort. The old adage "penny-wise and pound foolish" applies here. If a legitimate prospect is located across town or requires some special selling efforts, the professional must take the calculated risk that a sufficient number of such efforts will pay off.

One way to minimize expense is to prepare a prospect list within a defined trade radius. Once your radius has been established, however, initially treat all legitimate prospects equally. Many professionals get in the habit of calling only those prospects who are very close by or will see them at a convenient time. Once your list has been established, decide realistically how much time will be required to effectively work the list and what expenses will be associated with this effort.

EXPECTATION OF EARLY RETURNS

Closely related to the problem discussed in the preceding section is the unrealistic expectation on the part of professionals in working the prospect list. Don't decide (after much too short a period) that the sales being generated are insufficient or that substantial early returns should be realized. Nearly every article and book on selling ever written emphasizes that prospects offer several "No's" before becoming clients.

If the world's best sales professionals require many "No's" per prospect, is it realistic to assume that your selling efforts will require less to be successful?

INTEGRATE NEW LEADS AND DATA

The proper working of a prospect list often requires the passage of time. A frequent weakness in working a list is failure to integrate new leads and data in support of a list that has been prepared and is being worked. To combat this, the proper mind set must be established at the outset of the prospecting effort.

Maintain the notion that in the course of working the prospect list, new information may be gained that may have a substantial impact on the techniques and strategy you develop to penetrate this market. Sometimes you can learn something on the tenth call that is so important it's worth calling back the first nine prospects who conveyed little interest. Other times in working the list, information or leads are generated that make it worthwhile to alter your telephone presentation or, in rare instances, to forego working of the list for the time being. The important point is to recognize that the target market and your penetration efforts are both part of a dynamic environment that requires flexibility and often an updating of the list.

GET ORGANIZED AND STAY ORGANIZED

All other things being equal, the professional who takes the time to get organized and stay organized in working a prospect list will fare far better than one whose list and notes are in disarray, and who believes that taking 15 to 30 minutes a day to get organized is a waste of time. The time spent organizing one's files and notes is an investment that pays continuing dividends. This organization effort maximizes the prospecting effort. Although we can all cite instances in which unorganized professionals achieved some marketing success, the long-term odds are clearly in favor of those who invest at least a small portion of time in getting and staying organized.

THE PERSONAL TOUCH

The final key to a successful prospecting effort is to offer a personal touch. This, obviously, is best done by being face to face with the prospect. Direct mail (discussed in Chapter 14) has its place in support of the prospecting effort. When direct mail is used as a substitute for telephone contacts and personal presentations, however, a serious mistake is being made. If you've taken the time to define an appropriate target market, develop a prospect list, and sufficiently work a prospect list, why take shortcuts once the prospect has been qualified by using the mail instead of making a personal contact?

A systems analyst firm had decided to target several industries for special attention. Staff were given the vague instructions to "locate some warm bodies" within assigned industries. A large number of names was obtained, but new business never materialized because prospects were not contacted directly.

The active approach—making the personal contact (particularly for a second or follow-up visit)—is overwhelmingly more effective than the passive approach—using the mail.

A successful prospecting effort is analogous to litmus paper. The paper doesn't work until it's dipped, and the chances are your prospecting effort won't pay off unless you appear in person and reappear as often as necessary. Following the litmus paper analogy a step further, a chemistry takes place through personal contact between the prospect and you that simply doesn't exist by phone or mail.

This chapter has presented the elements of effective prospecting and that you ultimately have to "see them to sell them." Effective prospecting assures you that a healthy number of appointments can be made from which a relatively predictable sales volume can be generated.

You have now completed Part 1 on client-centered marketing, and are now ready for Part 2, on personal promotion, which encompasses Chapters 9 through 13.

PART
2

PERSONAL PROMOTION

THE NEXT step in the profitable marketing of professional and consulting services involves favorable promotion of *yourself* and your services. Promotion consists of the numerous activities involved in educating your targets, stimulating inquiries, and managing your image. Personal promotion consists of first-person activities that you undertake to favorably present your capabilities and ability to meet needs. Personal promotion is eye-to-eye or elbow-to-elbow contact and the use of personal letters that are action oriented.

The key objectives of promotion, based on principles of a client-centered marketing, leveraging approach are to:

☐ Favorably bring the firm's name before "targets of influence" and "targets of opportunity," and educate and inform same.

☐ Establish and maintain a sound and working relationship with the press and industry publishers of your target group and establish a reputation as an expert and willing source of information.

☐ Improve the firm's public and professional image by systematically gaining exposure for principals and professional staff in appropriate media.

☐ Develop and distribute client-centered, informative literature about the firm.

☐ Create a competitive difference by differentiating the firm's image with its targets.

☐ Stimulate and create inquiries from your firm's targets.

☐ Portray the benefits of your firm's services in an appealing fashion.

Many of the objectives should already be familiar to you as a result of the successful completion of Chapters 1 through 8. Chapters 9 through 13 focus on specific elements of effective personal promotion.

PERSONAL SELLING

PERSONAL SELLING in the context of client-centered marketing of professional services entails face-to-face discussions with prospective users, influencers, and purchasers of your services. Your personal selling objectives include (1) contacting and obtaining additional revenue from existing and prospective clients through discussion and identification of needs, (2) retaining endangered revenue with clients who may be thinking of terminating their relationship with you, and (3) obtaining referrals and leads from satisfied clients and targets of influence such as bankers.

Supporting activities to personal selling include responding to inquiries, maintaining control and awareness, acquiring keener listening skills, developing a personal image, and establishing proper "atmospherics."

This large and pivotal chapter provides answers to questions such as these:

☐ What is Robert Louis Stevenson's timeless quote on marketing (and *life*)?

☐   What is essential for a successful personal selling effort?
    (*Hint*: Belief in _____.)

☐   What are the steps to handling inquiries?

☐   How does personal control maximize personal selling efforts?

☐   Why don't we listen as well as we should? What can be done
    to improve?

☐   How do personal image and atmospherics affect professional
    success?

EVERYONE SELLS SOMETHING

Robert Louis Stevenson once said "Everyone lives by selling something," and although many professionals do not view themselves as
sales representatives, the function must nevertheless be fulfilled.

Effective personal selling requires that you have or develop the
willingness and ability to sense the unmet or poorly met needs of key
clients and prospects, probe for needed information without upset-
ting the contact, and listen to and understand the contacts' needs and
expectations. It also means that you communicate persuasively in
language the contact understands and, when appropriate, obtain
commitment to proceed to a logical next step in the business development process.

One key to successful personal selling is having a firm conviction
in your own capabilities. (Although the following may sound like a
pep talk, keep in mind that effective personal selling starts with a
proper frame of mind.) You may have superior technical knowledge,
but this alone is not enough. Belief in yourself is transmitted to your
clients and targets above and beyond what you say. Belief in yourself
is important, and without it the best trained and most professional
among us might as well seek another career. You must believe in
yourself and that you deserve to be financially rewarded for your
efforts. The enthusiasm you possess for your service is contagious;
moreover, it cannot be feigned on a sustained basis. If you don't be-

lieve in what you are selling, you can't possibly expect your client or target to do so—and they won't.

Robert Bookman, an Arlington, Virginia–based trainer and consultant, points out the power of belief in oneself combined with persistence. Every few months Bookman calls prospects just to stay in touch and maintain the potential for a professional relationship. In eight years of calling on targets he has never had anyone request that he stop calling them. Conversely, some of those called have since become clients.

RESPONDING TO INQUIRIES

A fundamental component in personal selling, and something that will occur with greater frequency after you employ the marketing and promotion techniques outlined in this book, is response to and handling of inquiries. Exhibit 17 carries you through the process.

EXHIBIT 17 RESPONDING TO INQUIRIES FROM EXISTING AND PROSPECTIVE CLIENTS

Handling the initial telephone contact

- ☐ Project an image of interest and enthusiasm
- ☐ Capture the contact's initial statement and attempt to identify the nature and scope of the need situation
- ☐ Gather additional background data
- ☐ Arrange meeting details

Planning for personal sales interview

- ☐ Organize your interview plan
- ☐ Select appropriate "marketing aids"
- ☐ Prepare yourself and others who may attend

EXHIBIT 17 (Continued)

Initiating the interview

- ☐ Make proper introduction
- ☐ Build rapport
- ☐ Read the contact's style and attitude

Defining the contact's need

- ☐ Determine the nature of the need situation, what's wrong, missing, required, or desired.
- ☐ Determine the scope of the need situation
- ☐ Determine the costs to date and the additional costs and consequences of not proceeding

Converting the need into goals

- ☐ Review *favorable circumstances* to be retained, enhanced, or created
- ☐ Identify *unfavorable circumstances* to be minimized or eliminated
- ☐ Determine timing and form of results required

Discussing solution alternatives and agreeing on a solution program

- ☐ You need . . . we could . . . we should . . . we will . . .

Handling contact's concerns and information needs

- ☐ Surface, define, resolve

Closing and seeking commitment

- ☐ Schedule meeting
- ☐ Prepare proposal, action letter, or plan
- ☐ Begin engagement

PERSONAL SELLING AND CONTROL

Personal control is a key element in successful personal selling. In personal selling, control of one's time, energy, and resources spells the difference between a halfhearted, limited-effectiveness sales effort and a professional, high-caliber approach.

Personal control goes hand in hand with personal awareness. There are three types of personal selling style in regard to the personal control and awareness functions: the no-control, nonaware salesperson; the no-control, aware salesperson; and the in-control and aware salesperson.

No Control, No Awareness

The professional service marketer with no control and no awareness doesn't plan in advance, yet expects to have a productive selling effort (see "Prospecting," Chapter 8).

No-control, nonaware marketers frequently let the effectiveness of their presentations slip. Rehearsals, brushing up, outside reading— all are relegated to the "haven't got time for that" status.

Professionals of this type are playing a loser's game, perhaps kidding themselves for an extended period or banking on a "long shot," the big contract that will salvage a poor month (or year!) This person is also the first to regard successful competitors as lucky or having the good "connections."

No Control but With Awareness

Many professional service marketers not adequately controlling their marketing effort are aware of the problem. These are people who either have let personal standards slip over the years or never adequately developed them. No-control but aware professionals often rationalize their reasons for skipping steps in the personal selling process. If you're in this category, supplement what you've learned in this book with attendance at outside seminars, specialized courses, and programs so that your approach to selling remains fresh and viable.

In Control and With Awareness

Professional service marketers in control and with awareness know each day and each week what they will be doing and where. They take time to review marketing strategies, rehearse presentations, and approach personal selling in a controlled and effective manner. This type of professional knows that taking the time to maintain personal control results in maximum presentation effectiveness and overall use of time.

The effective professional service marketer is eager to learn or read about successful sales strategies. This person welcomes luck but doesn't count on it and knows that a well-executed, sustained personal sales effort is the best road to increased revenues.

LEARNING TO LISTEN

Few professionals have thought about *learning* how to become a good listener. We get distracted when someone is talking, jump ahead in our minds to what we want to say next, and later blame the speaker for not getting the message across. Yet, a key tool of effective personal selling is the ability to listen.

According to researchers at the University of Minnesota, on the average, people spend 45 percent or nearly half of their communication time listening. Good listening is an active, complex process that takes knowledge of a few basic tenets and lots of practice. In a professional (or personal) relationship, it pays to sharpen listening skills.

Why don't we listen as well as we should? Dr. Chester L. Karrass, Director of the Santa Monica, California–based Center for Effective Negotiating, offers several reasons:

1. We often have a lot on our minds, and it's not easy to switch gears quickly to fully absorb and participate in what is being said to us.

2. We have adopted the habit of talking and interrupting too much and do not let the prospect continue even when it may be to our benefit.

3. We are anxious to rebut what the other person has said, and if we do not do so readily, we are afraid that we may forget to make our point.

4. We allow ourselves to be easily distracted because of the setting or environment in which the meeting takes place. Have you ever asked your secretary to hold all phone calls during meetings?

5. We jump to conclusions before all the evidence has been presented or is available.

6. We discount or "write off" some statements because we don't place importance on the party who is presenting them.

7. We tend to discard information that doesn't match what we want to hear or that we don't like.

Poor listeners may drop out of a conversation, erroneously thinking that they can catch up. Karrass observes that they seldom do.

YOU'RE NOT ALONE

If you're like most professionals, you may have self-confessed to being a poor listener. Lighten up—you don't have a monopoly on underdeveloped listening skills. Virtually all human beings must work to improve their listening skills.

Stuart L. Tubbs, of the General Motors Institute, believes that visual cues are highly influential in effective listening and interpersonal communication. Facial expression and eye contact are two of the most important visual cues. For example, if you avoid eye contact while listening, this could communicate disapproval or disinterest.

Even if you look directly at the prospect, your facial expression may still indicate a negative reaction. Tubbs points out that "probably the most rewarding combination is a smiling face and a head nod in combination with direct eye contact. From these and other cues we infer support, confirmation, and agreement." A good way to enhance one's listening capability is to pick a location and a time (when possible) that is free from noise and interference.

Here is a checklist developed by Dr. Richard C. Cupka of Purdue University to help you evaluate your own listening habits:

( )   Do you give the other party a chance to talk?

( )   Do you interrupt while the prospect or client is making a point?

( )   Do you look at the speaker while the person is speaking?

( )   Do you impart the feeling that your time is being wasted?

( )   Are you constantly fidgeting with a pencil or paper?

( )   Do you smile at the person talking to you?

( )   Do you ever get the prospect off the track or off the subject?

( )   Are you open to new suggestions or do you stifle them immediately?

( )   Do you anticipate what the other person will say next? Do you jump ahead anticipating what that person's next point will be?

( )   Do you put the prospect on the defensive when you are asked a question?

( )   Do you ask questions that indicate that you have not been listening?

( )   Do you overdo your show of attention by nodding too much or saying "Yes" to everything?

( )   Do you insert humorous remarks when the other person is being serious?

( )   Do you frequently sneak looks at your watch or the clock while listening?

This is a tough checklist, and every professional service provider will undoubtedly discover several areas for improvement.

Developing good listening habits is one way to become a better communicator. Active listening improves your interpersonal skills, human relations, and personal selling capabilities. Good listening skill can also enhance your professional life. The sooner you start listening effectively, the better!

Thousands of volumes have been written on personal selling, listening, and human relations. The following is a resource list (in no special order) of classics for newcomers as well as veterans to personal selling.

How to Use Tact and Skill in Handling People	Dr. Paul Parker
Get the Prospect to Help You Sell	Edward J. Hegarty
The New Art of Selling	Elmer G. Leterman
Secrets of Closing Sales	Charles B. Roth
How to Talk Your Way to Success	Harry Simmons
How to Sell When Selling is Tough	Elmer Wheeler
How to Sell Anything to Anybody	Joe Girard
The 5 Great Rules of Selling	Percy H. Whiting
How to Outsell the Born Salesman	Frank & Lupp
I Can	Ben Sweetland
Successful Salesmanship	Paul W. Ivey
How to Sell Well	James F. Bender
Keys to Modern Selling	Ralph G. Englesman
How to Win Friends and Influence People	Dale Carnegie
The Greatest Salesman in the World	Og Mandino
Winning Through Intimidation	Robert J. Ringer
Acres of Diamonds	Russell Conwell

YOUR PERSONAL IMAGE

We define "image" as the "sum total of all of the perceptions your clients and others have about you and your practice." Every element of your practice over which you have discretion will contribute to the development of an image. If that image is solidly developed and consistently displayed, the task of influencing your clients and targets will be greatly enhanced.

If your image is inconsistent or nonexistent, your marketing efforts will have to be all that much more strenuous. As Robert J. Ringer says in *Winning Through Intimidation*, "it's not what you say or do that counts, but what your posture is when you say or do it." Your clients and targets expect certain behaviors and characteristics of professionals in your field. Within this area of expectation, however, it is recommended that you develop your own unique image, for this is what will differentiate you from competitors. Back in 1978 Simon Ramo, empire builder and chairman of TRW, helped to build a unique personal image by becoming an avid amateur tennis player. He even wrote a successful book on the subject.

Since most readers wish to display a highly professional, somewhat conservative, polished image, the following items must be addressed:

1. *Wardrobe.* Read any issue of *Gentlemen's Quarterly* or *GQ* as it is now called. This is one of the best magazines published on the subject of professional (and leisure time) wardrobes.

2. *Logo, Stationery.* These must be tastefully designed and consistently applied to all of the firm's printed materials.

3. *Association Membership.* Successful professionals join and display the emblems of their industry associations (see section on Atmospherics, to follow).

4. *Community Relations.* Become involved with community, civic, and professional groups (see Chapter 10, on Leveraging your memberships).

5. *Your Receptionist.* This person must have a pleasant, commanding speaking voice and know how to property convey the firm's desired image.

This list is by no means comprehensive but is presented to stimulate your awareness of image-related factors. Throughout this book, keep in mind that your image and your firm's image, whether clearly spelled out or heretofore unknown or unrecognized, will color the perception of your clients and targets with virtually the same impact as your verbal or written message.

It is difficult to consistently maintain a false image or one that is beyond your area of personal comfort. If you seek to change your image, recognize that the process will take some time. As Earl Nightingale says, initially you'll have to "act the part." Eventually, you can embrace and maintain that image which you desire.

An image and atmospheric self assessment checklist is presented in Exhibit 18.

ATMOSPHERICS

Your clients and office visitors are exposed to elements of your image when visiting your office. Your office's atmospherics—that is your personal image as reflected in your office—speak loudly.

For example, the types of magazine you display reveal something about your firm. If *National Geographic, Scientific American,* or *Psychology Today* or some type of international magazine is displayed, you convey a "global," intellectual, perhaps philosophical approach to business and the image that certain coveted achievements and milestones have perhaps already been reached. If *Forbes, Fortune,* and similar publications are displayed, visitors perceive a fair degree of success and an image of at least a moderate level of sophistication. If you display *Time, Newsweek, Business Week,* or *US News and World Report* the background or interest of the firm

EXHIBIT 18   ASSESSING YOUR IMAGE AND ATMOSPHERICS

Image	
Wardrobe	
Suits	Blue, gray, and beige are best, 100% wool or a wool/polyester blend. Solids, subtle plaids, tweeds, pinstripes. Ladies—brown, camel, maroon, and black colors also OK.
Shirts	White, light blue; and blue, maroon, beige, or brown pinstripe on white. Ladies—much greater color assortment.
Ties	Silk, or polyester that looks like silk, cotton or wool. Avoid any odd or garishly colored or designed tie.
Shoes	Black, brown, cordovan. Slip on, lace, wingtips. Ladies—add gray and blue.
Socks	Dark colors, over the calf. Ladies—flesh-colored pantyhose.
Belts	Black or brown, avoid fancy buckles. Ladies—in vogue with season.
Coat	Blue, camel. Ladies—add gray, not too dressy.
Attache case	Dark brown or cordovan.
Glasses	Nontinted with dark rims.
Jewelry	Thin, gold, never loud or brassy.
Personal	
Grooming	Short hairstyle, neatly trimmed beard or moustache. Sideburns according to latest trend. Fingernails—clean, short. Ladies—moderate length hairstyle; fingernails—professionally manicured in appearance.
Accessories	Pens—silver or gold Cross. Pipe, cigar, cigarettes (avoid if possible).
Automobile	Late model, noncompact car, clean, dent free. Noncluttered and in top operating condition.

EXHIBIT 18 (Continued)

Image (blank form)

Wardrobe

Suits _____
_____
_____
_____

Shirts _____
_____
_____

Ties _____
_____

Shoes _____
_____

Socks _____
_____

Belts _____
_____

Coat _____
_____

Attache case _____
Glasses _____
Jewelry _____

Personal

Grooming _____
_____
_____
_____
_____

Accessories _____
_____

Automobile _____
_____
_____

EXHIBIT 18   (Continued)

Atmospherics

Building

  Exterior
    Appearance <u>OK—older building in downtown area</u>
    Outdoor sign <u>Not applicable</u>
    Parking <u>Very difficult</u>
    Neighborhood <u>Appropriate</u>

  Lobby
    Decor <u>Fair—needs modernization</u>
    Signage <u>OK— white lettering on black template</u>
    Cleanliness <u>Clean, but with poor lighting looks worse</u>

Offices

  Interior—Reception Area
    Decor <u>OK-could use new drapes and fixtures</u>
    Layout <u>A little cramped</u>
    Screening <u>Good - other offices are not visible</u>
    Displays <u>**Good—association plaques, our brochure, &** Fortune</u>
                                               magazine
  Interior—Offices, Hallway
    Cleanliness <u>Good</u>
    Illumination <u>Good but fixtures are old</u>
    Decor <u>Fair</u>
    Density <u>Hallways are not wide, offices are OK</u>

Staff

  Professional Staff
    Dress <u>Excellent—pin stripes, conservative, fashionable</u>
    Demeanor <u>Professional at all times</u>
    Other <u>Appear active, busy</u>
  Support Staff (i.e., Receptionist)
    Dress <u>Excellent</u>
    Demeanor <u>Perhaps too young to convey desired image</u>
    Attentiveness <u>OK</u>

EXHIBIT 18 (Continued)

Atmospherics (blank form)

Building

Exterior
Appearance _____
Outdoor sign _____
Parking _____
Neighborhood _____

Lobby
Decor _____
Signage _____
Cleanliness _____

Offices

Interior—Reception Area
Decor _____
Layout _____
Screening _____
Displays _____

Interior—Offices, Hallway
Cleanliness _____
Illumination _____
Decor _____
Density _____

Staff

Professional Staff
Dress _____
Demeanor _____
Other _____

Support Staff (i.e., Receptionist)
Dress _____
Demeanor _____
Attentiveness _____

are not necessarily reflected. If *Life, People,* or *Sports Illustrated* are displayed, it's more than likely for the reading enjoyment of the visitors but may not convey the image you desire.

SHOW US YOUR PLAQUES

Be sure to display any trade association plaques or membership certificates. Older, more established professional service firms usually belong to at least one trade association and display the plaque proudly. The plaque often indicates the year you joined, which delivers a message to visitors.

It is probably best to shield your offices from the reception area. Firms that have high regard for their employees and are trying to convey a sophisticated image shield employees from view.

It is acceptable and, in fact, recommended to display company literature. Visitors often read any brochures that are available, and if they can't read them before speaking to you, they read them afterwards.

Chapter 10 expands on the strategy of leveraging your memberships.

10

LEVERAGING
YOUR MEMBERSHIPS

V ISIT ANY city in the United States and attend a local meeting of the Heart Association, United Way, American Cancer Foundation, or other civic or charitable groups and undoubtedly, you will meet many of the area's most successful professionals. Successful professionals know that giving of their time freely is an excellent way to be of service to the community and to help build the firm. After completing this chapter, you'll know:

- [ ] Why it is important to join charitable and civic organizations.
- [ ] The names of at least three national groups that have chapters in your area.
- [ ] The key criterion for joining an organization.
- [ ] Why joining any organization will be fruitless if you do not meet and remember targets of opportunity and influence.

EARNING A POSITION OF LEADERSHIP

Civic organizations such as the Chamber of Commerce, Scouts, and the YMCA afford professionals ample opportunity to rub elbows with key community and business leaders and jointly work on solving local, civic, public, and business problems. In marketing your professional services it is often assumed that you are fully competent in your practice area. The important thing is getting known throughout the community and getting known among your peer group in other professions. Earning a position of leadership in a high-visibility organization is an excellent way to be of service and, as a by-product, promote your services. By volunteering your services and assisting civic and charitable organizations, targets of opportunity, and influence come to know you as a person and then feel comfortable in using you as a professional or in referring your services to others.

Joining and serving can only be effective if you "pay the price" required to gain a leadership position in the organizations and associations in which your *targets* belong. You are leveraging off the organization and the lead time necessary to begin to receive "benefits" can range from 6 to 18 months. Many professionals don't stand their ground, drop out, and never realize that benefits of leveraging were just "around the corner."

An unsophisticated marketer joined an organization and unrealistically expected to generate new business simply as a result of attending various meetings and becoming known. After nearly two years he resigned his membership and concluded that joining organizations "just isn't for me."

A resourceful consultant joined an organization comprised of decision makers in her targeted prospective client organizations. She sought and was appointed to the new member committee. Serving in this capacity, she met all new members, and during the course of the screening, interviews, and subsequent new member activities, developed sound relationships that eventually led to opportunities to discuss ways of serving them.

JOINING WITH A PURPOSE

Memberships in professional and civic activities need to be closely monitored to determine whether marketing results in addition to personal satisfaction are being achieved. Otherwise, joining can be a serious drain on the firm in terms of time and energy. Because every community is different and the interplay of political, social, cultural, and religious spheres varies from time to time, a customized joining–serving strategy must be prepared.

It is essential for professionals to continually analyze organizational contacts for relationships that should be developed, paying particular attention to younger executives on their way up. This approach must be balanced, however, with the realization that the only organizations that one should join are those in which one has a genuine interest and desire to serve.

Numerous strategies abound for the successful penetration of charitable and civic organizations. One way is to seek specific offices. For example, the role of activities chairman is a coveted position in many groups because one can gain a high degree of visibility and have virtually unlimited access to key people in one's market and practice area.

If there are two to three or more partners in your firm, you can match partners' personal interest with the firm's goals. Thus Jones may join A, B, and C groups, whereas Brown joins D, E, and F. You may choose to join C, F, and G, thereby increasing your firm's visibility in organizations C and F and maintaining some visibility in all seven.

If you do not meet and remember targets of opportunity and influence and they do not remember you, the act of joining any organization will be fruitless from a marketing standpoint. Some professionals maintain card files on individuals when a key contact is made. Information is continuously added to the card file as it is obtained.

Making targets of opportunity and influence remember you is a delicate matter. The best way is to respond professionally and completely when asked about your profession and not to "oversell." If your commitment to and involvement with a charitable or civic association is extensive, you may rightly expect that you will become known and remembered by many of the right people.

GROUPS, ANYONE?

Why not take the time right now to identify six organizations in your community that interest you:

Active Corps of Executives
American Business Women's
   Association
American Cancer Society
American Heart Association
American Legion
Boys' Club
Business and Professional
   Women's Club
Catholic Youth Organization
Chamber of Commerce
Children's Hospital
   Committees
Democratic Party
Easter Seal Campaign
Elks
Fraternities (professional)
Garden Club
Goodwill Industries
Historical Society

Independent Party
Jaycees
Jewish Community Center
Kiwanis
Lions
March of Dimes
Masons
Optimist Club
Parent-Teacher Association
Public Television
Regional Park Authority
Republican Party
Rotary Club
Salvation Army
Scouts of America
Toastmasters
United Way
Volunteer Services
Walkathon
YMCA, YWCA

This list offers the names of groups that may commonly be found in your area. A local phone call will yield membership information.

Chapter 11 focuses on leveraging associations in a different way: speaking to them!

<u>11</u>

SPEAKING:
AN UNDERUSED,
UNDERVALUED TOOL

MANY LOCAL organizations such as the Small Business Administration, Community Colleges, and civic and charitable associations actively seek speakers. Yet the program chair of these groups often must scramble to find an interesting speaker. If you give a good presentation as a volunteer speaker to local groups, and are in fact able to influence the audience, rest assured that you'll be contacted by individual members at some point in the future regarding professional services. In this chapter you'll discover:

☐   What is the best way to position yourself to be invited to an organization.

☐   What type of letter should be sent describing your topics.

☐   What tips should be followed to increase your effectiveness.

☐   Why you should make sure your presentation is taped.

☐   Why you should always provide "handouts" for the audience.

POSITIONING TO SPEAK

The best way to position yourself to be invited to speak to a local organization is to be a member of that organization. This strategy ties in with the need to join charitable and civic associations.

The authors have consistently applied this principle and in the last year we have spoken to the following groups, of which one or both of us are members:

Institute of Management Consultants

Washington Independent Writers

Greater Washington Society of Association Executives

Active Corps of Executives

American Marketing Association

National Capital Speakers Association

SPREADING THE WORD

An excellent way to spread the word that you are available for seminar presentations is to type a one-page letter explaining who you are, a little about your background, and a one-line or short paragraph description of three to five topics on which you are prepared to speak. This letter could easily be photocopied and distributed by your clerical staff to 50 to 100 groups in the local area. As a result of this mailing and depending on how well known you are in the community, two to five speaking engagements may be generated. A sample letter appears in Exhibit 19.

EXHIBIT 19   SAMPLE SPEAKER'S LETTER

Alvin I. Speakeasy
Consultants Unlimited
10 Orator Avenue
Wichita Falls, TX
(   ) 444-4444

Dear Meeting Planner:

Your organization may have need for a speaker with my experience and qualifications. I am a management consultant serving businesses and government agencies since 1974. I have had numerous speaking engagements and written several articles on effectively managing a business.

My most frequently requested topics are:

How to trim expenses when there's nothing left to trim
Developing a management style
How to attract, motivate, and retain young executives
Starting your own business
The record-keeping aspects of managing your own business
How to stand up to the IRS
Eight ways to save on advertising expense
Common mistakes of successful business professionals
Incorporating a firm
Cash flow analysis for short-term planning
How to find the right consultant for your business
Analyzing your business's debt capacity
How to prepare a loan package

Your interest is appreciated. Feel free to call me at the number above to discuss any of the topics listed.

Yours truly,

Alvin I. Speakeasy

For this or any other mailing, it is wise to send a second letter or to have someone on your staff make a follow-up phone call to each of the organizations receiving your letter. This reinforces your desire to speak.

HONING YOUR EFFORTS

When you start to get requests to speak, you will need additional information such as the size and setup of the meeting (see Exhibit 20). A checklist of items you should find out about to increase your effectiveness on the day or night of your presentation is given in Exhibit 21.

OPENING NIGHT

Here are some guidelines for making your presentation.

1. *Posture* should be erect and poised.
2. *Hand gestures* should be made mainly between the shoulder and the waist and be appropriate to the material presented.
3. *Body movements*, if made, should be stable and appropriate to the material.
4. *Vocal production* must be audible to the size of the audience.
5. *Vocal intonation* should be varied.
6. *Vocal rate* should be appropriate to the size of the audience and the material presented.
7. *Articulation* must be clear and precise.
8. *Delivery* should have few or be absent of audible pauses.
9. *Eye movement* should make contact regularly with the audience.
10. *Approaching and leaving* should be deliberate.

EXHIBIT 20 MEETING ROOM SETUP

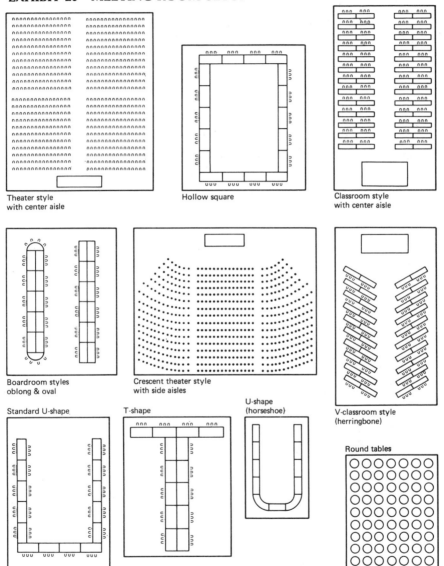

Theater style
with center aisle

Hollow square

Classroom style
with center aisle

Boardroom styles
oblong & oval

Crescent theater style
with side aisles

V-classroom style
(herringbone)

Standard U-shape

T-shape

U-shape
(horseshoe)

Round tables

EXHIBIT 21   CHECKLIST FOR EFFECTIVE SPEAKING ENGAGEMENT

☐	Size of room	☐	Audiovisual equipment
☐	Setup, staging	☐	Surrounding rooms
☐	Number of attendees	☐	Temperature
☐	Program length	☐	Lighting
☐	Sound system	☐	Audience composition

GET YOUR SPEECH ON TAPE

Every speaker should insist on being taped while making a presentation to a live audience. Why? There are five reasons:

1. *Taping Affords Personal Review of the Presentation.*   There is no better way to review your performance than to hear exactly what you said and how you said it, on tape.

2. *Each Tape Is Potentially Salable.*   Tape cassette producers, manufacturers, and distributors can professionally edit your tape, supplying voiceovers, and transition passages that can result in a salable cassette. Keep in mind that there are other audiences similar to the one to whom you spoke. It may pay for you to be able to repeat your presentation on tape.

3. *The Tape Transcript Is Salable.*   Don't overlook the value of marketing the tape transcript to members of the group you addressed. Professional societies frequently offer tape transcripts from symposia and seminars that they have sponsored to those members who were not able to attend or who wish to have a written record of what was said in the speech.

4. *The Transcript Can Be Converted into Articles.*   Frequently, a transcript of as few as three or four pages lends itself to being turned into an excellent article. Every writer finds it easier to start from an established base and make editorial changes than to face four blank pages and begin writing. With longer transcripts,

it may be possible to extract several excellent articles, which in turn can be used to promote your speaking career and earn additional income.

5. *Use Tapes to Get Other Speaking Engagements.*   After your speaking engagement has been taped, you can extract a 5- to 10-minute passage that can be used to develop demonstration tapes for distribution to other meeting planners. What better way for them to assess your speaking skills than to hear a passage from a live performance?

HELPING THE AUDIENCE TO REMEMBER YOU

Distribution of article reprints or other written material along with the speaking engagement "provides the audience with an opportunity to secure the correct name and address of the speaker." Thus it always makes good sense to hand out something with your presentation. On the other hand, don't attempt to make a sales pitch or sales presentation; merely speak on a topic of interest and do your best. Never expect a speech or presentation to bring instant results. Altman and Weil, a professional services consulting firm, reports that it received telephone calls from targets who heard a member of the firm speak several years previously.

Your decision on whether to seek speaking engagements as a personal promotional tool hinges on your ability to be interesting and have something worthwhile to say to a group composed of targets of opportunity and/or influence. If you've never spoken before a group, you have a unique experience in store. Everyone is nervous at first, but shortly you may find speaking quite exhilarating. Before going on to Chapter 12 (on action letters) on a separate sheet of paper make a rough copy of your own speaker's letter, modeled after Exhibit 19. Then turn it in for typing, because it's ready for mailing!

12

CLIENT-CENTERED
ACTION LETTERS

T HE MANAGEMENT action letter is becoming increasingly important in the professional–client relationship and, since it either immediately precedes or follows a personal selling opportunity, is included (as is Chapter 12, on proposals) in Part 2, on personal promotion.

The development of client-centered action letters that display the same level of quality as the rest of your professional services is the key to effective use of this personal, promotional tool. This chapter provides you with the answers to these questions:

☐ Why are most letters written from the wrong perspective?

☐ How could these statements be changed to reflect a client-centered approach?

"When we examined the Northside Branch we observed that X,Y,Z . . . ."

"We feel that our recommendations for an improved reporting system have not been followed."

☐ Are your clients more inclined to take action because your letter suggests action that will provide an acknowledged benefit, or because they'll be operating in accordance with "generally accepted procedures"?

☐ What type of letter headings are most likely to gain client cooperation?

PUTTING YOUR LETTERS IN PERSPECTIVE

Most management action letters are written from the perspective of the professional who develops them. This is because it's easier to write from one's own perspective.

For example, an account executive with an aggressive advertising agency in the Midwest took an "audit" of his management action letters. He relates that "I was appalled at the 'I'-centeredness of my letters—"I will send you . . ." rather than "You will receive . . . ," and so on. "I also found that I tended to 'push' services we provide rather than suggest solutions to actual client needs."

A good way to calculate the effectiveness of a management action letter is to count the number of times "I" or "we" is used rather than "you" or the equivalent appears. The following excerpts are from actual letters. The first set indicate the "I/we" orientation, which should be avoided:

1. "In *our* review, *we* noted the poor control in data processing . . . ."

2. "*Our* personnel had to develop schedules to assist X, Y, Z . . . ."

3. "*We* are pleased to inform you that *our* recommendations made . . . ."

Here is how each example can be changed to convey the same meaning with the use of a client-centered approach:

1. *"Management* will want to improve controls in the data process-ing area . . . ."

2. *"Management* could realize reduced costs if *internal personnel* are used to develop schedules which X, Y, Z . . . ."

3. "The *sales staff* is to be complimented for greatly improv-ing . . . ."

You'll find that the client-centered management letter will be more readily accepted by the client and enhance your relationship.

USE THE CLIENT'S LANGUAGE

Client-centered management action letters should influence the client to change because of the benefits that will be derived, and not because the client will be operating in accordance with some generally accepted procedure or standard. Here are two excerpts from actual manage-ment letters used by professionals in correspondence with clients:

1. "Better standards of documentation should be adopted imme-diately to conform with the guidelines established in QRS Com-pany's specification manual."

2. "The company does not maintain a fixed asset ledger as is normal procedure for an organization the size of GHI Corporation."

This terminology should be restated, using client-centered termi-nology so that the benefits of the recommendations being made are clearly spelled out. The preceding passages could be rewritten thus:

1. "Better standards of documentation will assure the company of uninterrupted operations in the event of a sudden turnover in personnel."

2. "The company could benefit in two ways if a fixed asset ledger were developed and maintained: (a) you would reduce the risk of

losing valuable assets, and (b) you would be better able to determine the most favorable methods of depreciation for tax purposes."

HEADINGS THAT SUGGEST ACTION

The client-centered management letter can also be used in other ways to win the client's cooperation. Find a letter that you recently sent, and compare the number of headings and subheadings relating directly to your services. The headings might be:

Advertising	Data collection
Insurance	Payroll
New Products	Inventory

Now consider varying your headings in a way that would arouse interest. For example:

Advertising effectiveness	Improving your management
Maintaining full insurance	information system
coverage	Reducing payroll costs
Establishing a climate for	Improving inventory control
new innovations	

MORE READABLE LETTERS

Here are other suggestions to make your management action letter more readable and useful to the client. Mark weaknesses that are uncorrected items from the previous management letters. Then indicate to the client that the operating efficiency of the company is contingent on its ability to correct these weaknesses. Another technique is to provide space for an "Action taken" column so that your clients may check off those areas in which corrective measures are taken.

If possible, deliver the action letter in person. This helps to build the professional–client relationship and increases the client's propensity to follow the suggestions you have given in the letter.

Here are three ways to determine whether your procedure for developing action letters yields a good-quality letter. First, does the time charged to letter writing frequently overrun original budget estimates or fees that exceed estimates given to clients? Second, are management action letters written and submitted on a timely basis or long after services have been provided (and in the case of a prospective client, long after the initial discussion)? Finally, have guidelines been established to ensure that letters are carefully edited and that the final message is appropriate and on target?

Every letter (including nonmanagement action letters) that you send to a client or target of influence "carries promotional weight." Seek opportunities from the very beginning of your professional relationships to use action letters to best advantage. Later, standard letters can be developed and used for routine events such as greeting new clients, thanking targets of influence for referrals, and reminding clients of deadlines, opportunities, and the like.

Samples of two new business analyses made by an accountant in Denver that led to increased business from existing "A" clients are given in Examples 1 and 2.

Through observation, data collection, and follow-up, the accounting firm influenced a client to purchase additional services:

Example 1

Observations: Inventory turnover in the last five years had decreased from nine times a year to four times a year. The company was experiencing an inventory buildup and cash shortage even though sales had increased steadily over the years.

Data Collection: An examination of the available inventory data and inquiry of management revealed the following:

No substantial improvement in the level of customer service has been achieved by the buildup in inventory.

The company had a problem with obsolescence of inventory (items had been bought in greater quantities than needed to achieve price breaks).

Buying decisions were made without adequate emphasis on inventory management.

Management Letter: Communicated to management the benefits to be achieved from an automated purchasing system integrated with the inventory system.

Result: The accounting firm was engaged to develop and install a system to assist buyers, based on certain inventory management criteria.

Example 2

Observations: The client had separate bank accounts for separate operating units. Some accounts had large cash balances, whereas others had overdrafts (suggesting an opportunity for better cash management).

Data Collection: An examination disclosed that there were bank charges on some accounts and cash lying idle in others, and that over a dozen operating units were writing separate checks to the same vendors each month.

Management Letter: Communicated to management the potential benefits of consolidating payables into a single account and using an improved accounts payable automated system. This would (1) pool cash, (2) reduce bank charges, (3) provide better cash management, (4) provide revenue from the excess cash, (5) decrease clerical effort, and (6) organize the payables procedure. (The recommendations emphasized *the benefits* to be achieved rather than the problems diagnosed.)

Result: After receiving a favorable response from the client, the accounting firm proposed an engagement to install an improved, automated accounts payable system utilizing a central bank account and pooled cash funds. This proposal was accepted.

A checklist summarizing the elements of effective client-centered management letters is provided in Exhibit 22.

EXHIBIT 22 CHECKLIST FOR EFFECTIVE CLIENT-CENTERED MANAGEMENT ACTION LETTERS

Have you reduced the "we" orientation of letters and complimented clients where possible?

Have you stressed the benefits of implementing recommendations instead of recanting established procedures?

Have you organized management letters by area of client interest instead of by your industry's terminology?

Have you established guidelines that provide realistic estimates of the time required to develop a top-quality letter?

The use of management action letters expanded to proposals is discussed further in Chapter 13.

13

CLIENT-CENTERED PROPOSALS

AN INCREASING number of clients and prospective clients are asking professional service firms to prepare proposals as a prerequisite to initiating an engagement. A proposal can be viewed as a logic extension of a management action letter.

The key to writing a successful proposal is to obtain current information on the nature, scope, and needs of the target or a particular solicitation and to present information within the proposal in a manner that convinces the target that hiring your firm represents the best way to accomplish the task. Yet, writing a superior proposal will never substitute for effective personal selling. This chapter will enable you to answer these questions:

- ☐ What is a proposal?
- ☐ What are the sections contained in an effective proposal?
- ☐ How does the client-centered proposal process work?

☐　Why should marketing efforts to any target precede proposal writing?

WHAT IS A PROPOSAL?

A proposal is a document that sells a target on the basis of your firm's ability to perform specified services. The proposal must indicate that your firm understands their needs and has the willingness, facilities, human resources, management experience, and track record to support the tasks to be performed, minimize the burden on the client, and ensure that the delivery of services or final product is of high quality.

Proposals can be seen as being comprised of seven sections, including the following:

1. *Background Information.*　This brief section introduces who is proposing what to whom. It may also reflect some prevailing conditions or important observations.

2. *Statement of the Problem.*　This section provides at a minimum a brief history of the need or problem as diagnosed by the proposal writer and the occurrences or events that led up to the present situation. The concluding paragraph in this section should highlight the objectives of the proposed engagement and might quite literally begin with the phrase "Our objectives in undertaking this assignment" or "We hope to accomplish. . . ."

3. *Methodology or Approach to Be Followed.*　This section highlights the underlying rationale for the activities, steps, and/or procedures that you feel are necessary and proper in the professional execution of the proposed engagement. This is an important section because the client must comprehend and agree with your approach to solving the problem as defined in the previous section as a prerequisite to initiating the engagement.

4. *Scope of Work.*　This section spells out the precise tasks and subtasks that you propose to undertake, including their initia-

EXHIBIT 23 MONTHLY WORK PLAN

Examination Area ╲ Months	1	2	3	4	5	6	7
Management Plan	▲						
Task 1	├——▲						
Task 2		├———▲					
Task 3			├———▲				
Task 4				├———▲			
Task 5					├——▲		
Final Report					├———▲		
Monthly Summary of Activities	▲	▲	▲	▲	▲	▲	▲

▲ Deliverable.

tion, sequence, and completion time. This section is traditionally bolstered by a program evaluation and review technique (PERT) chart or other supporting exhibits that illustrate to the client your proposed tasks chronologically (see Exhibit 23).

5. *Expected End Product.* This section is generally brief and concise. It describes what the client can expect as a result of being provided your services. It also helps to alleviate any client misconceptions as to what services and what results should be expected.

6. *Management and Staff Resources.* This section introduces and describes the project director, who has overall responsibility for the successful execution of the project and has the power and authority to redirect, extend, or otherwise represent the firm per contractual agreement; the project manager, who is responsible

for the day-to-day control and management of the project, continuing client liaison and handling of all staff assigned to the project; and project staff, who may be called on to perform various professional services. This section is traditionally bolstered by a project organization chart, a staff days allocation chart, and biography sketches or resumes (see Exhibits 24 and 25).

EXHIBIT 24   TYPICAL PROJECT ORGANIZATION

EXHIBIT 25   PROJECT STAFF DAYS

Tasks \ Title	Project Director	Project Manager	Associates	Staff Consultant	Total
Management plan	4	8	3	—	15
Task 1	2	20	12	6	40
Task 2	4	32	28	16	80
Task 3	2	16	14	8	40
Task 4	5	24	12	9	50
Task 5	2	20	12	6	40
Final report	2	9	4	—	15
Monthly summary	2	8	3	—	13
Total	23	137	88	45	293

7. *Cost.* This section is sometimes referred to as the *cost* proposal and is delivered as an attachment to the main body of the proposal. This section includes an elaboration of all direct labor costs, other direct costs, labor overhead rate, general and administrative expenses (that can be billed to the client, if so agreed), travel expenses, profit or fee, and total project cost. This section is supported by detailed line extensions and summaries of all cost categories. Footnotes to the cost computations are also given, including cost reduction activities such as use of client office, space, and equipment.

THE CLIENT-CENTERED PROPOSAL PROCESS

Now let's examine the client-centered proposal process and how it contributes to the submission of an effective, on-target proposal. The first step (see Exhibit 26) is handling the initial contact. This includes defining the client's perception of the need situation, probing for information that you must have in order to fully understand the situation, and nurturing the climate in which both you and the client will freely and openly discuss expectations. It is in this first crucial area that a "go–no/go" decision must be made.

If a "go" decision is made, the next step is to develop a client-centered data bank. This means assembling data or information that enables you to understand the nature of the client's organization, market, and industry (see Chapter 5, on researching markets). You must then organize your experience in handling this particular client need situation.

The third step in the process is to plan for the initial meeting. Spell out your meeting objectives. Also, prepare a meeting guide that includes information that must be obtained, information that must be verified, and any supporting props or presentation materials that you must bring. The roles and responsibilities of your proposal team should also be determined during this planning session.

The next step in the client-centered proposal process is to conduct the initial meeting with the client as a prelude to proposal preparation.

EXHIBIT 26   CLIENT-CENTERED PROPOSAL PROCESS

1. *Handle initial contact*
   Define client's perception of
   need situation
   Surface expectations
   Probe for "must-know"
   information
   Make "go–no/go" decision

2. *Develop client-centered data
   bank*
   Learn the nature of client's
   organization, market, and
   industry
   Organize your experience in
   handling need situation

3. *Plan for initial meeting*
   Establish objectives
   Prepare meeting guide
   Information to verify
   Information to obtain
   Evidence to bring along
   Define role(s) and responsi-
   bilities of proposal team

4. *Conduct initial meeting*
   Verify preinterview research
   Define situation
   Surface expectations

5. *Prepare client-centered
   proposal*
   Assign responsibilities
   Schedule worksteps
   Prepare outline
   Expand outline with first
   draft
   Review draft with "murder
   board"

6. *Review and present proposal
   to client*
   Schedule meeting
   Rehearse presentation
   Identify likely questions
   Conduct presentation
   Seek commitment to proceed

7. *Follow up as required*
   Assess situation
   Assign responsibilities
   Make contacts
   Determine reasons for win-
   ning (or losing)

During this meeting you should verify your preinterview research and more precisely define the need situation with the client. At this time you should again seek to bring both your and client expectations to the surface so that both parties are working in synchrony.

The next step is preparation of the client-centered proposal following the seven proposal sections as outlined earlier in the chapter.

An effective technique for ensuring proposal success, however, is to review both your proposal outline and first draft with an in-house "murder board." The murder board can consist of staff or associates that closely scrutinize and criticize every component of the proposal. This will greatly strengthen your final product to be delivered to the client.

The next step will be to present the proposal to the client and review all questions and concerns. You may wish to rehearse your presentation and identify likely questions in advance. If you are going to be assisted in your proposal presentation, the presentation roles and responsibilities should be worked out in advance. The presentation should be client centered—proceeding at the speed in which the client can comprehend what is being proposed. Your goal is to obtain the client's approval and commitment to the project so that you may initiate the engagement in a timely manner.

A final step could be called *follow-up*, in which the overall situation is assessed, responsibilities assigned, and key contacts made. It is at this time that you should also reflect on your reasons for winning (or losing) this bid for new or additional business.

One consulting engineering firm is in the practice of calling its marketing team together to assess the operations in the areas of proposal preparation and presentation. The team leader asks each member to answer the following questions:

1. What was the "tie breaker" in each winning situation?

2. What percent of submitted proposals won in each of the functional disciplines? Was there a consistency in the wins for each area?

3. To what extent did the oral presentation play a role in the situations in which they did not succeed?

4. Is the competition doing something new or different?

Lively and penetrating analysis then ensues.

TIPS FOR SUCCESS

The proposal is a key marketing tool of the trade. Proposal development and submission can be a costly process; thus an internal system for identifying where and when proposals will be written must be established. Although writing a good proposal cannot in itself secure new business, writing a bad one can surely result in loss of business.

The format and packaging of the proposal often play a significant part in influencing the target that a service is needed or that your firm represents the best of all firms submitting proposals.

The target is generally concerned with the professional's knowledge of the specific industry, previous or present clients served in that industry, and the personnel who will be directly engaged on the project. One expert notes that the prospect "will ordinarily have only marginal interest in a professional's firm history, organization or training programs." A small engagement may require a proposal that is merely an elaborate action letter and only a few pages in its entirety, whereas a large engagement may require 20, 30, or 40 pages. In any case, proposals should contain as much information as needed to cover all important points effectively and efficiently. [*Note*: Appendix B continues with proposals submitted in response to request for proposals (RFPs).]

Unfortunately, many professionals begin their real marketing efforts when they start work on the proposal, whereas marketing efforts should be initiated long before. Your *ongoing* efforts to favorably influence targets of opportunity and influence is part and parcel in the development of a successful proposal. In the final analysis, the best proposal is no proposal, because you're wired!

You have now completed Part 2 on personal promotion, and are ready to tackle Part 3 on nonpersonal promotion, which is presented in Chapters 14 through 19.

PART
3

NONPERSONAL
PROMOTION

THE MARKETING and promotional tools of the trade discussed in this section should be used in direct support of the client-centered marketing approach and as a complementary or alternative vehicle to personal promotion. A wide variety of promotional tools exist including direct mail, writing and using articles, using the local press, advertising, and brochures.

Effective but costly or time consuming promotional vehicles that have been used by large firms have been omitted or discussed only briefly because the time and effort required for the smaller practitioner to develop a client newsletter, for example, is generally prohibitive. Marketing and promotional tools of the trade (nonpersonal) that have proved effective and are readily implemented by successful smaller practices are presented in the chapters that follow. The order in which these vehicles are discussed does not reflect their importance or potential effectiveness for your firm.

14

USING DIRECT MAIL

DIRECT MAIL is a unique form of promotion because the letter or message that you enclose can be personalized and distributed to targets of opportunity. Direct mail is flexible in that you can control the timing and scope of the effort. However, the preparation of effective direct mail correspondence often requires the assistance of other professionals. In this chapter we discuss ways direct mail can be used and sources available to you. Specifically, you'll be able to answer the following questions:

☐ What are some of the benefits of using direct mail?

☐ In what ways can lists be subdivided and precisely targeted to suit your needs?

☐ What is the cost range for a 1,000-name mailing list?

☐ What are three local sources that can be used to develop a mailing list?

THE MAILING CYCLE

Many firms have successfully used direct mail and are in the habit of making specialized mailings throughout the year (see Exhibit 27). For example, the distribution of professional holiday greeting cards is a standard in many industries and represents a simple form of direct mail. It's a nice gesture to send holiday greeting cards to clients, associates, nearby businesses, and friends to let them know that you remember them, that you are in practice, and that you truly wish them well.

EXHIBIT 27   MONTHLY MAILING THEMES

Month	Theme(s)
January	New Year's
	End of tax year
	Physical examination
February	Presidential sales
March	Getting ready for spring
April	Income tax returns
	Increase daylight hours
May	Spring cleaning
June	Graduations
July	Independence Day
August	Dog days of summer
September	Labor Day
	Back to school
	Recharge efforts
October	Beginning of government fiscal year
November	Harvest
	Thanksgiving
December	Holidays
	Reduce inventory
	Time off

Some firms purchase lists or use in-house developed lists for a special mailing to coincide with the year's end and start of the new year. Such mailings emphasize the firm's ability to provide assistance in the year ahead. Bulk rate mail permits can be obtained from your local postal office to enable you to greatly reduce mailing costs.

Larger firms have found that the compilation of mailing lists is a key element in the development and growth of the practice. For targeted industries in which you have particularly strong experience, you may decide to experiment with the use of mailing lists to see what your returns are. If you have strong experience with advertising agencies, for example, you could order a mailing list through a list compiler that provided the names of thousands of advertising agencies across the country.

FOCUSING IN ON YOUR TARGETS

If you wish to focus more narrowly on your state, region, or metropolitan area, you're in luck, because major list compilers offer this capability. Research Projects Corporation, for example, offers the following special selections:

State Selection	Net Worth
City Metro Area Selection	Financial Rating
Test Cross Sections	SIC Code
Title Addressing	Occupational Title Selection
Number of Employees	Other Special Selections
Sales Volume	Related Services

To continue with our example, within the area of advertising agencies, the Research Project Corporation maintains a list of 19,000 advertising agencies and counselors, 27,000 advertising agency executives, 3,600 major advertising agencies, and 3,000 advertising agency presidents.

The cost for purchase of a mailing list generally ranges from $30 to $100 per 1,000 names. Virtually all mailing list compilers rent their list for one-time use only, unless otherwise stated. Many provide outright sales of the mailing list for unlimited use within a designated period of time—often one year. Under this arrangement the cost of the list is understandably much more expensive than for one-time use.

INFORMATION SOURCES

If you're interested in pursuing direct mail as a marketing vehicle for your firm, the following sources of information will be useful:

Research Project Corporation
4 South Pomperaug Avenue
Woodbury, Connecticut 06798
(203) 263-0100
Toll-free number (except New York) (800) 645-2980

This mailing list supplier has been in business since 1951.

List Research Letter
Agora Publishing
2201 Saint Paul Street
Baltimore, Maryland 21218

This newsletter, costing approximately $200 per year, presents information regarding the validity and effectiveness of various mailing lists available nationally.

Direct Mail/Marketing Association, Inc.
6 East 43rd Street
New York, New York 10017

The Direct Mail Marketing Association provides support, information, and guidance in the application of effective direct marketing techniques.

National Business Lists, Inc.
162 North Franklin Street
Chicago, Illinois 60603

(312) 236-0350
Toll-free number (800) 221-1599

> National Business Lists, in business for over 25 years, specializes in the compilation of business, professional, and institutional lists representing a data base of over 10 million names.

Daly Associates, Inc.
918 16th Street, NW
Washington, DC 20036
(202) 659-2959

> Daly Associates provides communication, counseling, and direct mail or marketing assistance, and offers a free catalogue describing several "tipsheets" on direct mail, including one that answers the most common questions asked.

R. L. Polk and Company
6400 Monroe Boulevard
Taylor, Michigan 48180
(313) 292-3200

> Now in its 115 year, Polk offers an awesome 85-page catalog describing direct mail lists and capabilities.

The managing partner of a firm that had made no use of direct mail decided to investigate the use of the tool. He asked several of his clients for the names of their direct mail consultants and talked with others to obtain ideas and names of possible suppliers. He asked the suppliers what direct experience they had in creating direct mail campaigns for similar firms.

For suppliers who passed the first hurdle, he then asked: "How much time do you estimate that it would take you to learn specifically about us and develop a central theme and cost-effective campaign for building name recognition and stimulating inquiries?"

Only the firms that pointed out the futility of such a campaign were asked to submit a proposal for building a continuing direct mail campaign for the firm to accomplish the primary goal of taking the "chill" out of the initial telephone contact.

DEVELOPING YOUR OWN LISTS

There are numerous other sources from which target lists can be generated:

1. Your local Yellow Pages directory
2. The roster of members of the local Chamber of Commerce
3. Attendees at trade shows
4. Newspaper advertisers
5. Blue and red books or other commercial directories

The cost of compiling these lists, developing targeted letters and other information, and mailing should be weighed against the potential for developing new business. Traditionally direct mail campaigns generate a 1 to 2 percent return, although this return can be greatly exceeded if bolstered by follow-up telephone calls, additional mailings, and adherence to the client-centered, leveraging, marketing approach.

15

WRITING AND USING ARTICLES

YOUR FIRM can enjoy a large number of benefits when you have an article printed in a business or professional publication. There are also, however, some misconceptions about what getting published will do for the firm. Unfortunately, the misconceptions often diminish the positive net benefit that getting published provides because of high author expectations. In this section we examine the benefits that getting published does and does not provide. We also discuss getting mentioned in articles and using someone else's article to reinforce a point you'd wish to make to a client. The questions to be addressed include:

☐ What are some of the primary benefits of getting published?

☐ What are the secondary benefits of getting published?

☐ What are the best topics for articles?

☐ How can one easily overcome writers' block and start writing?

125

☐   What place does getting an article published have in your
    overall marketing effort?

☐   How can you get mentioned in the articles others are writing?

PUBLISHING OPPORTUNITIES ABOUND

The number of general, industrial, business, professional, and in-
house publications has risen dramatically in the last 10 years. By using
Bacon's Publicity Checker, Working Press of the National, the
Writer's Market, Ayers Publications Directory, or *Gebbie's All in
One Directory*, you can obtain the name, address, telephone number, editorial content, fees paid, circulation, target audience, and
submission requirements for over 10,000 journal magazines!

There are also over 6,500 newsletters in the United States today,
and the number is growing at an exponential rate. The *Oxbridge
Directory of Newsletters* is particularly useful. Publication within
newsletters may yield the same actual benefits as can be achieved
through publication in the larger trade magazines. The net benefits
for you and your firm, of course, are contingent on the match between the target market of the newsletter and your targets of opportunity and influence. A partial list of professional magazines and
journals is given in Exhibit 28, and a list of regional business tabloids
is presented in Exhibit 29. For a magazine or a journal, ask for a sample issue to review, and later write to the editor to relay your article
theme.

EXHIBIT 28   PROFESSIONAL MAGAZINES AND JOURNALS

ABA Banking Journal
Simmons-Boardman Publishing
  Corp.
345 Hudson Street
New York, NY 10014

Accounting Review
American Accounting Association
5717 Bessie Drive
Sarasota, FL 33583

Across The Board
The Conference Board, Inc.
845 Third Avenue
New York, NY 10022

American Demographics
P.O. Box 68
Ithaca, NY 14850

*American Journal of Small
  Business*
University of Baltimore
School of Business
1420 N. Charles St.
Baltimore, MD 21201

Appraisal Journal
American Institute of Real Estate
  Appraisers
450 N. Michigan Ave.
Chicago, IL 60611

Association Management
American Society of Association
  Executives
1575 Eye Street, NW
Washington, DC 20005

Business Horizons
Indiana University
Graduate School of Business
Bloomington, IN 47401

Business Marketing
Crain Communications, Inc.
740 Rush Street
Chicago, IL 60611

Cashflow Magazine
1807 Glenview Road
Glenview, IL 60025

CPA Journal
New York State Society of
  Certified Public Accountants
600 Third Avenue
New York, NY 10016

Credit & Financial Management
National Assn of Credit
  Management
475 Park Avenue South
New York, NY 10016

Engineering News-Record
P.O. Box 430
Hightstown, NJ 08520

Financial Analysts Journal
Financial Analysts Federation
1633 Broadway, 14th Floor
New York, NY 10022

Financial World
250 Broadway
28th Floor
New York, NY 10001

Harvard Business Review
Soldiers Field
Boston, MA 02163

*Hospital & Health Services
  Administration*
American College of Hospital
  Administration
840 North Lake Shore Drive
Chicago, IL 60611

EXHIBIT 28 (Continued)

In Business
J. G. Press, Inc.
Box 323 18 S. 7th St.
Emmaus, PA 18047

Inc.
38 Commercial Wharf
Boston, MA 02110

Industrial Engineering
Technical Services Department
Institute of Industrial Engineers,
 Inc.
25 Technology Park/Atlanta
Norcross, GA 30092

Institutional Investor
Institutional Investor, Inc.
488 Madison Avenue
New York, NY 10022

Journal of Advertising
Anthony F. McGann
The University of Wyoming
Box 3275, University Station
Laramie, WY 82071

Journal of Business
Graduate School of Business
University of Chicago
5836 S. Greenwood Avenue
Chicago, IL 60637

Journal of Business Strategy
Warren, Gorham & Lamont, Inc.
210 South Street
Boston, MA 02111

Journal of Marketing
American Marketing Association
250 South Wacker Drive
Chicago, IL 60606

Journal of Marketing Research
American Marketing Association
250 South Wacker Drive
Chicago, IL 60606

*Journal of Organizational
 Behavior Management*
The Haworth Press, Inc.
38 East 22nd St.
New York, NY 10010

*Journal of Small Business
 Management*
West Virginia University
Bureau of Business Research
Morgantown, WV 26506

Journal of Systems Management
Association for Systems
 Management
24587 Bagley Road
Cleveland, OH 41338

Manage
National Management Association
2210 Arbor Blvd
Dayton, OH 45439

Management Accounting
National Association of
 Accountants
919 Third Avenue
New York, NY 10022

Management Review
American Management
 Association
135 W. 50th Street
New York, NY 10020

Managerial Planning
Planning Executive Institute
Box 70
Oxford, OH 45056

EXHIBIT 28 (Continued)

Managers Magazine
LIMRA
P.O. Box 208
Hartford, CT 06141

Marketing Times
330 West 42nd St.
New York, NY 10036

Modern Office Technology
Penton-IPC
1111 Chester Avenue
Cleveland, OH 44114

National Public Accountant
National Society of Public
  Accountants
1010 N. Fairfax St.
Alexandria, VA 22314

Personnel
American Management
  Association
135 West 50th Street
New York, NY 10020

Personnel Administrator
American Society for Personnel
  Administration
30 Park Drive
Berea, OH 44017

Personnel Journal
245 Fisher Ave, B-2
Costa Mesa, CA 92626

Practical Accountant, The
Institute for Continuing
  Professional Development, Inc.
964 Third Avenue
New York, NY 10022

Public Relations Journal
Public Relations Society of
  America
845 Third Avenue
New York, NY 10022

Sloan Management Review
Massachusetts Institute of
  Technology
50 Memorial Drive
Cambridge, MA 02139

Supervisory Management
American Management
  Association
135 West 50th Street
New York, NY 10036

Tax Adviser, The
1211 Avenue of the Americas
New York, NY 10036

Training
Lakewood Publications, Inc.
731 Hennepin Avenue
Minneapolis, MN 55403

Training & Development Journal
ASTD Suite 305
500 Maryland Ave., SW
Washington, DC 20024

Venture
35 West 45th Street
New York, NY 10036

Working Woman
Dept MWMUI
P.O. Box 10130
Des Moines, IA 50349

EXHIBIT 29   REGIONAL BUSINESS TABLOIDS

Pacific

Alaska Business & Industry
P.O. Box 10 3036
Anchorage, AK 99510
(907) 561-1932 (M, $25)

Oregon Business
1515 Southwest 5th Avenue,
   Suite 875
Portland, OR 97201
(503) 228-1332 (M, $18)

Seattle Business Journal
1008 Western Avenue, Suite 415
Seattle, WA 98104
(206) 583-0701 (W, $52)

California Business
6420 Wilshire Blvd, Suite 711
Los Angeles, CA 90048
(213) 653-9340 (M, $15)

Los Angeles Business Journal
3727 W. 6th Street
Los Angeles, CA 90020
(213) 385-9050 (W, $26)

San Diego Business Journal
3444 Camino del Rio N
San Diego, CA 92108
(619) 283-2271 (W, $26)

San Francisco Business Journal
745 Stevenson Street
San Francisco, CA 94103
(415) 552-7690 (W, $26)

Hawaii Business
P.O. Box 913
Honolulu, HI 96808
(808) 946-3978 (M, $18)

Pacific Business News
P.O. Box 833
Honolulu, HI 96808
(808) 521-0071 (W, $31)

The Business Journal—San Jose
1435 Koll Circle, Suite 112
San Jose, CA 95112
(408) 295-3800 (W, $26)

Mountain

Colorado Business
P.O. Box 5400-TA
Denver, CO 80217
(303) 295-0900 (M, $24)

Denver Business
899 Logan St., Suite 307
Denver, CO 80203
(303) 832-5400 (M, $28)

Rocky Mountain Business Journal
1590 S. Federal Blvd
Denver, CO 80219
(303) 934-2411 (W, $26)

New Mexico Business Journal
P.O. Box 1788
Albuquerque, NM 87103
(505) 243-5581 (M, $21)

Phoenix Business Journal
1817 N. 3rd St.
Phoenix, AZ 85004
(602) 271-4712 (W, $27.30)

Canada

Atlantic Business
3030 7001 Mumford Road
Halifax, Nova Scotia B3L4R3
(902) 455-6335 (6×, $12)

EXHIBIT 29 (Continued)

B.C. Business
601 510 W. Hastings St.
Vancouver, B.C. V6B1L8
(604) 689-2021 (M, $17.95)

Manitoba Business
874 330 Graham Avenue
Winnipeg, Manitoba R3C 4A5
(204) 944-1441 (6×, $12)

Saskatchewan Business
199 N. Leonard Street
Regina, Saskatchewan S4N 5X5
(306) 949-6666 (6×, $12)

Montreal Business
1440 Ste. Catherine St. West
Montreal, Quebec H3G 1R8
(514) 879-4014 (6×, $13.50)

Northern Ontario Business
158 Elgin St.
Sudbury, Ontario P3E 3N5
(706) 673-5667 (M, $9)

West North Central

Corporate Report Minnesota
7831 E. Bush Lake Road
Minneapolis, MN 55435
(612) 835-6855 (M, $21)

Minnesota Business Journal
7831 E. Bush Lake Road
Minneapolis, MN 55435
(612) 835-6855 (M, $18)

Minneapolis Citibusiness
100 N. 7th St.
Minneapolis, MN 55403
(612) 333-3717 (BW, $20)

St. Louis Business Journal
712 N. 2nd St.
St. Louis, MO 63102
(314) 421-6200 (W, $25)

Corporate Report Kansas City
4149 Pennsylvania
Kansas City, MO 64111
(816) 931-4541 (M, $9)

Kansas City Business Journal
3543 Broadway
Kansas City, MO 64111
(816) 561-5900 (W, $26)

Kansas Business News
P.O. Box 511
Lindsborg, KS 67456
(913) 227-3330 (M, $15)

Western Business
P.O. Box 31678
Billings, MT 59107
(406) 252-4788 (M, $27)

West South Central

New Business
201 Jefferson Street
Lafayette, LA 70502
(318) 233-7484 (M, $25)

New Orleans Citibusiness
3900 N. Causeway Blvd.,
   Suite 1111
Metairie, LA 70002
(504) 834-9292 (26×, $30)

Baton Rouge Business Report
P.O. Box 1949
Baton Rouge, LA 70821
(504) 387-5000 (M, $22)

EXHIBIT 29 (Continued)

Journal Record
621 N. Robinson
Oklahoma City, OK 73102
(405) 235-3100 (D, $98)

Tulsa Business Chronicle
P.O. Box 1770
Tulsa, OK 74102
(918) 581-8560 (W, $30)

San Antonio Executive
1603 Babcock Road, Suite 159
San Antonio, TX 78229
(512) 341-0110 (M, $8)

Texas Business
5757 Alpha Road, #400
Dallas, TX 75240
(214) 239-4481 (M, $16)

*Dallas-Fort Worth Business
  Journal*
11300 N. Central Expressway
Dallas, TX 75243
(214) 692-5846 (W, $26)

Houston Business Journal
5314 Bingle Road
Houston, TX 77092
(713) 688-8811 (W, $26)

West Texas Business
P.O. Box 1367
San Angelo, TX 76902
(915) 655-6154 (M, $8.50)

East North Central

Crain's Cleveland Business
140 Public Square, Suite 412
Cleveland, OH 44114
(216) 522-1383 (W, $25)

Ohio Business
Suite 425, Hanna Building
Cleveland, OH 44115
(216) 621-1644 (M, $24)

Indiana Business
9302 N. Meridian Street,
  Suite 248
Indianapolis, IN 46260
(317) 844-8627 (M, $12)

Indianapolis Business Journal
3500 DePaul Boulevard,
  Suite 2111
Indianapolis, IN 46268
(317) 872-8101 (W, $25)

Crain's Chicago Business
740 N. Rush Street
Chicago, IL 60611
(312) 649-5358 (W, $32)

Crain's Illinois Business
740 N. Rush Street
Chicago, IL 60611
(312) 649-5358 (Q, $10)

Wisconsin Business Journal
450 N. Sunnyslope Road,
  Suite 120
Broomfield, WI 53005
(612) 941-5820 (M, $26)

LaCrosse Citibusiness
421 Main Street
LaCrosse, WI 54650
(608) 782-2130 (M, $15)

East South Central

Advantage
1200 Fidelity Federal Building
Nashville, TN 37219
(615) 256-1973 (M, $15)

EXHIBIT 29   (Continued)

Mid-South Business
4515 Poplar, Suite 232
Memphis, TN 38117
(901) 685-2411 (W, $18)

Mississippi Business Journal
P.O. Box 4830
Jackson, MS 39216
(601) 981-9401 (M, $15)

Tennessee Business
c/o Advantage
1200 Fidelity Federal Building
Nashville, TN 37245
(615) 256-1973 (6×, $23)

Louisville Magazine
300 W. Liberty
Louisville, KY 40202
(502) 582-2421 (M, $16.50)

New England

New Hampshire Business Review
36 Warren Street
Concord, NH 03301
(603) 228-0472 (M, $9)

Vermont Business World
On the Square
Bellows Falls, VT 05101
(802) 463-9933 (M, $12)

Boston Business Journal
P.O. Box 72, Back Bay Annex
Boston, MA 02117
(617) 268-9880 (W, $35)

Business Worcester
P.O. Box 1000
Worcester, MA 01614
(617) 792-3800 (M, $12)

New England Business
31 Milk Street
Boston, MA 02109
(617) 482-8200 (22×, $15)

Connecticut Business Journal
P.O. Box 487
Harnson, NY 10528
(203) 622-1220 (W, $21.95)

Middle Atlantic

Capital District Business Review
105 Wolf Road
Albany, NY 12206
(518) 458-7000 (M, $9.95)

*Central New York Business
  Review*
5858 E. Molles Road, Suite 119A
Syracuse, NY 13211
(315) 454-3201 (M, $9.95)

Long Island Business
303 Sunnyside Boulevard
Plainview, NY 11803
(516) 349-8200 (W, $49)

Westchester Business Journal
P.O. Box 487
Harnson, NY 10528
(914) 835-4600 (W, $21.95)

New Jersey Success
One Evans Terminal
Hillside, NJ 07205
(201) 352-3282 (M, $16)

Corporate Monthly
(formerly Delaware Valley)
105 Chestnut Street
Philadelphia, PA 19106
(215) 629-1611 (M, $18)

Focus Philadelphia
1015 Chestnut Street
Philadelphia, PA 19107
(215) 925-8545 (W, $45)

EXHIBIT 29　(Continued)

Philadelphia Business Journal
2300 Market Street
Philadelphia, PA 19103
(215) 569-0202 (W, $25)

Pittsburgh Business Journal
7 Parkway Center, Suite 270
Pittsburgh, PA 15220
(412) 922-2404 (W, $26)

Pittsburgh Business Times
100 Wood Street
Pittsburgh, PA 15222
(412) 391-7222 (W, $25)

South Atlantic

Maryland Business Journal
7 Church Lane
Baltimore, MD 21208
(301) 484-4300 (6×, $12)

Baltimore Business Journal
131 E. Redwood St.
Baltimore, MD 21202
(301) 576-1161 (W, $20)

Regardie's
1010 Wisconsin Avenue
Washington, DC 20007
(202) 342-0410 (6×, $30)

Washington Business Journal
6862 Elm Street, Suite 430
McLean, VA 22101
(703) 442-4900 (W, $26)

Washington Business Review
P.O. Box 587
Vienna, VA 22180
(703) 281-4681 (W, $24)

Business North Carolina
314 S. Tryon Street
Charlotte, NC 28202
(704) 372-9794 (M, $15)

Charlotte Business Quarterly
P.O. Box 221269
Charlotte, NC 28222
(704) 375-8034 (Q, $8)

Business Atlanta
6255 Barfield Road
Atlanta, GA 30328
(404) 256-9800 (M, $15)

Atlanta Business Chronicle
1740 Century Circle
Atlanta, GA 30345
(404) 325-2442 (M, $15)

Independent Professional and
　Florida Business Journal
P.O. Box 13485
Gainesville, FL 32604
(904) 371-2900 (24×, $22)

Florida Trend
P.O. Box 611
St. Petersburg, FL 33731
(813) 821-5800 (M, $18)

Tampa Bay Business
P.O. Box 24185
Tampa, FL 33623
(813) 877-6627 (W, $24)

South Florida Business Journal
3785 NW 82nd Avenue, Suite 204
Miami, FL 33178
(306) 594-2100 (W, $26)

Miami Review
100 NE 7th Street
Miami, FL 33101
(306) 377-3721 (D, $78)

Other U.S.

Caribbean Business
P.O. Box 6253, Loiza Station
San Juan, Puerto Rico 00914
(809) 728-3000 (W, $25)

BENEFITS OF GETTING PUBLISHED

The primary benefits of getting published include the following:

1. Building the firm's reputation.
2. Establishing your credentials.
3. Creating a favorable impression.
4. Bolstering the firm's marketing tools.
5. Providing or generating inquiries.
6. Being invited to speak to groups.

Let's examine each benefit in detail.

Getting published *establishes credentials* for you and your firm in the article topic area. If a partner in an engineering firm, for example, writes an article on reinforcing bridge supports, a public notice has been made that the firm has expertise in this area and may provide assistance in this area. A similar example can be drawn for nearly any topic.

You can *create a favorable impression* when supplying associates with a reprint of an article you have had published. Modesty aside, most authors are very proud of their work and have no qualms about submitting reprints to friends, relatives, and associates, and most business associates will be pleased and impressed to accept your article reprint. Although they may not say so directly, they may also revel in your small glory and serve as an ambassador for you by informing others.

Many firms maintain a notebook in reception areas that include the articles and publications of their employees. The articles discuss a wide variety of topics within the fields of specialization. Visitors to the office are impressed by the writing skills and subject expertise of the company staff.

Another benefit of getting published is that the publication or article reprint helps *bolster your firm's brochures and marketing portfolios*. You can include reprints in all your correspondence, including proposals. An article reprint also increases the effect of a direct mail campaign.

The placement of articles in professional or trade journals may provide or generate *inquiries from potential clients*. After a writer from a local public relations firm has published an article in the Sunday edition of the newspaper (perhaps in the business and finance section or in the style sections), some phone calls and inquiries may be generated as a result of the article. For magazine publications, readership response to the article is less clearly defined. However, some readers viewing the article may (1) clip or photocopy the article for future reference and (2) contact you for further information, comments, or to seek assistance.

A final benefit is that an article will often result in your *being invited to speak* before a particular group. In actuality, every article can be made into a speech and vice versa. Thus the opportunity to repeat your message locally to defined markets should not be overlooked.

HOW TO DEVELOP ARTICLE TOPICS

The best topics for articles are derived from the successful *work that you have already done*. This may include reports, papers, summaries, guides, exhibits, and so on that you previously presented to a client, which can be generalized and applied to a larger audience. You may wish to write an article *with* a client for whom you have produced exceptional results.

Other good topics for articles include those topics that can be addressed by you or any members of the staff. If you're an architect, you may have an excellent article on "tips for success when designing skywalks" in your mind, even though you may never have written about the topic. *Any topic* that can readily be addressed by you or your staff and is of interest to your selected market is a good topic.

If you are developing your credentials in a specific market or functional area, then, by all means, a topic in that specified market or area on which you can intelligently write is an excellent one on which to write. This represents hard work but will be worth the effort. An article that stresses client benefits received as a result of working with you is particularly useful.

GENERATING ARTICLE TOPICS

Here are some ways to generate article topics and enable you to get started on the high road to getting published:

1. Make a list of gripes or discomforts in connection with your profession. It matters not where you work or what you do—a list of gripes can readily be created. Within each gripe lies the seed of a subject for an article. If something bothers you, it undoubtedly bothers others in your field. Discuss the problem in broad industry terms and offer suggestions for redress. The authors have done this on several occasions on the topics of management, marketing, and starting new ventures. By recognizing the universality of a problem that you face in your profession, you will instantly be creating material for an excellent article.

2. Start a clip file of articles that interest you. Every time you read the Sunday newspaper or a professional journal, save those articles that strike your fancy. You need not even know what you'll be using the article for. File all the clippings by topic or subject area. Months later, review your clip file, and to your amazement you will see that what you've clipped serves as the catalyst for numerous article ideas. Freelance writers have successfully used the clip file technique for years.

3. Develop a list of 6, 8, or 10 ways to do something better. The market for "how-to" articles seems to be increasing steadily as more and more clients thirst for "do-it-yourself" information. By introducing a number into the title of the article, such as "Eight Ways to Accomplish XYZ," you have established a hook that will strike the fancy of your selected target market. Take some

time right now or after finishing reading this chapter to draw up some lists of ways to do something better. The "number" can be assigned when you run out of ways. Thus "Eight Ways to Do Something Better" could be changed to "Six Ways to Do Something Better" if you can't come up with the additional two. You'll still have an interesting article and one that will be published.

4. Recall your favorite professional experience, most unforgettable character, biggest disappointment, or other memorable event. If you've been practicing for more than a year, undoubtedly you will have a number of interesting experiences, and these make good starting points for articles.

5. Shorten or adapt larger articles, reports, or papers that you've already done. The fastest way to write an article is to not write— to glean the essence of previous work, update it, improve it, or prepare it from a different perspective. We've gone back through old consulting reports and quickly found two that could be readily converted to publishable articles.

Here's a checklist of the ideas mentioned above for generating article topics:

Make a list of new developments in your profession.

Start a clip file of articles that interest you.

Make a list of 6, 8, or 10 ways to do something better.

Recall your favorite professional experience, most unforgettable character, biggest disappointment, and so on.

Review previous reports, outlines, papers, summaries to determine whether an article can be developed.

OVERCOMING WRITER'S BLOCK

Many professionals who want to write an article never do so for a variety of reasons. If writer's block is a problem, and you can't assign the task to a staff member or can't afford to hire an outside writer, the following suggestions may help you get started:

1. Create a one-page outline of an article idea. Over the years, we've found that producing a one-page outline or as little as 10 key words on a page was more than sufficient as guidance through the preparation and completion of an article. Devote an entire day to simply preparing article outlines or chronological sequences that can later serve as useful tools when you're ready to write the full-blown article. The technique of using an outline or one-page list works well because only a 5- to 10-minute time investment is required. Later, when you have time available to write the article, you will find that the outline keeps you on track and hastens efficient manuscript completion.

2. Think about how the phrase "published author" will look on your brochure. By visualizing the rewards of writing and getting your article published, you can break out of the chains that may currently restrain you and get started on an article that you can finish *today*.

3. Avoid extraneous reading. Think of all the times that you read the newspaper and within three days totally forgot 95 percent of what you read. Analyze what the continual reading of the paper has done for your income, career, and life in general, and you might agree, at least somewhat, that you could skip reading the paper now and then, write more articles, and enjoy the benefits of getting published. Recall the last time you read in detail of a large airplane crash or the problems of individuals in government offices. Topics such as these serve as headlines to major newspapers time after time. What real impact do they have on your life and career?

4. Clear your desk of everything except what you need to write your article. People have trouble writing often because their desk is a mess and not conducive to creativity. Recognize that during the time you're preparing an article you must tune out distractions. An effective way to do this is to work on a clear surface.

5. Identify in advance the target audience that will be interested in reading your article. If you can concentrate for a moment on who will be reading your article and what impact it will have on them, the task of completing your article will flow more smoothly. Think of the last time you wrote a letter to a friend or relative and how easily the words and ideas flowed. Your writing task was on a one-to-one basis, and your target audience was perfectly defined. You can achieve the same effect when you precisely define the target group that will be reading your article. If it's helpful to you, you might write the names of your target group on the top of your outline (e.g., "Peers," "Associations," "Executives Earning Over $60,000 Per Year").

6. Write for five minutes and see what happens. Forget all the excuses, all the reasons why you don't feel like writing now, or why it wouldn't be a good time to write. Sit down, place your watch in front of you, and start writing for a timed five minutes. Often you will find that you don't wish to stop after five minutes. Getting started is the key obstacle to writing productively. If you can master the "five-minute technique," you will develop a habit that will blast the term "writer's block" out of your vocabulary. The five-minute technique is so effective that even if you cannot complete the article at the initial sitting you undoubtedly will finish faster and more easily than you would have otherwise.

AN ALTERNATIVE: INFORMATION BOOKLETS

A useful alternative to writing articles is to publish and distribute an information booklet. A possible title could be: "Facts on Closely Held Corporations," "Tips on Stretching Advertising Budgets," or other literature of general interest to your targets. In no way does this have to be a comprehensive dissertation. However, your targets realize that it is best to hire competent professionals. Thus you can distribute a small information booklet that will be read and will prompt people and firms to contact you. Management consultants, lawyers, and engineers have all successfully distributed "facts-on" booklets.

Here's a checklist for overcoming "writer's block" when attempting to write:

- ☐ Create a one-page outline of an article idea.
- ☐ Think about how the phrase published author will look on your brochure.
- ☐ Avoid extraneous reading; instead, write your article.
- ☐ Clear your desk of everything except what's needed to write your article.
- ☐ Identify in advance the target audience that will be reading your article.
- ☐ Try writing for five minutes and see what happens.
- ☐ Develop an "information booklet" as an alternative.

Most professionals find that once they get started, writing an article is not a difficult task.

GETTING MENTIONED IN ARTICLES

Getting mentioned in articles by others is simple to describe but arduous to undertake. Identify the names of all local and national reporters writing in publications you've targeted, and send them a package of information on *you*. If you maintain contact on a quarterly or semi-annual basis, the odds are that within a year at least one of the many writers on your list will contact you for quotes, observations, or lengthier interviews. (Also, refer back to Chapter 7, on cultivating referrals.) Doing excellent work for clients also helps because your clients may offer your name to reporters when the opportunity arises.

To make this strategy work, you'll have to identify at least 25 writers. Also, the information you send them must be clear and concise and illustrate or describe your expertise in your field of endeavor.

Remember, getting an article or several articles published or being mentioned in an article *will not serve as a substitute for a comprehensive marketing program*. The articles will serve to supplement a good marketing program but will not, by any means, replace it. Also, the *positive effects of getting an article published are largely temporary*. For six or nine months, you may benefit by being published, but in this age of information and information overload, an article dated March 1986 has less and less impact as 1987 draws near. In combination with the effective use of other marketing tools, a published article can provide useful benefits, indeed.

USE SOMEONE ELSE'S ARTICLE

Finally, consider using an article written by someone else (in which you're not mentioned). If you wish to make an important point to a client, use data, quotes, or studies that support your proposal or service suggestion. For instance, a consultant obtained permission to duplicate an article that summarized the eight key factors found in successful organizations by Peters and Waterman. The consultant sent an accompanying letter to prospects that said, "I disagree with two of the factors discussed in the article and have discovered another factor not identified by the authors. If you would like to discuss your situation and receive a brief description of the 'ninth factor,' I'd be delighted to hear from you."

In Chapter 16 we explore other ways to leverage your marketing efforts through the local press.

USING THE
LOCAL PRESS

AN EFFECTIVE method of marketing and promoting a professional practice is through the use of publicity and the local press. Effective publicity and public relations can contribute to your overall marketing effort at little or no cost and in many cases can be more effective than paid advertising and the publicity that paid advertising may "buy."

Fortunately for the small practitioner, the generation of publicity does not require substantial time or effort. What is required is familiarity with techniques designed to generate publicity and implementation of those techniques with which you feel comfortable.

In this chapter you'll gain answers to the following questions:

☐ What is publicity?
☐ What is a news release?
☐ Who can submit news releases?

☐ What are good topics for news releases?

☐ What are some other techniques for using the local press?

PUBLICIZE, PUBLICIZE

For many professionals a sustained advertising campaign is beyond the resources of the firm. Through an effective public relations campaign and the generation of publicity, however, it is possible to use media sources, particularly the local press, to keep your name in front of targets of opportunity.

Public relations involves all planned activities undertaken to influence public opinion. Publicity is a key component of public relations and has been defined as media coverage of events, including background information, descriptions, relevant data, or other current information involving an individual, product (or service), business, or organization.

Contemporary society is media "oriented." Thus one article or news release about you in the local paper can generate more publicity, for example, than an exhaustive, expensive direct mail campaign. The easiest and least expensive way to use the local press is through preparation and submission of news releases. (Also refer back to the section in Chapter 15 on how to get reporters to interview you.)

NEWS RELEASES TO MEDIA

You can submit a news release—that is, information about your firm —to newspapers and radio at no cost and obtain free publicity. Some of the items that make good press releases include promotions of individuals within the firm, the hiring of new personnel, where you will be speaking, contract awards received, relocation or renovation of your offices, results of surveys you've completed, and expansion of your services. Each of these items is sufficient information to make

EXHIBIT 30 GOOD TOPICS FOR NEWS RELEASES

Services

New clients

Studies you've completed

Office expansion, renovation, relocation

New service introduction

New uses for existing products

Lower cost due to more efficient operation

Unusual service offerings

Bids or awards

New contracts

Firm

Affiliations

Accomplishments

Anniversaries of firm, principals, or long-term employees

Association memberships

New building or radical change in office layout

Banquets or awards dinners

Employee training programs

Projected plans

Joint programs—government industry

Promotion

Contests, new offers, premiums

Exhibits, trade show, display

Promotion success story

Visits by notable individuals

Overcoming competitors

New design, trademark, logo

New market areas—industry, geography

Employees

Speaking engagements

Reprints of speeches

Travel abroad

Interesting backgrounds, hobbies

Noteworthy accomplishments of employees

Increase in employee benefits

Employee awards

Retirements, births, deaths

Civic activities

Courses completed, certificates, citations, degrees

Seminars attended

Publications—books, articles

Community Activity

Fund-raising events

Program sponsorship, i.e., scholarships to foreign exchange, internships

Memorial, dedication or testimonial ceremonies

Training community labor force

Local news that relates to company

Community exhibits in which company has taken part

Local election to office of company official

Meeting announcements

Research

Survey results

New discoveries

Trends, projections, forecasts

New equipment or facility development

a good news release. A more comprehensive list of news release topics is presented in Exhibit 30.

Read your local newspaper today and you will undoubtedly spot two or three news releases about professionals in your area. It might concern an engineering or architectural firm but the release will state the name of the firm, the location, what they do, and probably a quote from one of the principals.

All that is required to have that information in the newspaper is to type up a short, one- or two-page sheet and submit it to the city editor with details regarding whom to contact if follow-up information is desired. Sending a good photograph never hurts. (But don't expect its return!) Remember, there is no "roving reporter." To get a news release published, *you* must develop and send it! A sample is provided in Exhibit 31.

NEWS RELEASE FOLLOW-UP

After submitting your news release, you should undertake the following activities:

NEWS RELEASE FOLLOW-UP

It's no typographic error; after you submit a news release to an editor, do nothing. If your release is run, you'll know soon enough. Your associates, friends, and relatives will be calling! However, it is not wise or recommended that you:

Call the editor.

Ask for clippings.

Seek a publication date.

EXHIBIT 31   SAMPLE NEWS RELEASE

George Franks and Company
West Haven Professional Building
Pasadena, California
(818) 888-8888

FOR IMMEDIATE RELEASE
Contact: Sue Powell
888-8888

PASADENA ARCHITECT EXPANDS OFFICE

George Franks and Company, an architectural firm practicing in the Pasadena area for the past four years, recently moved its office to the West Haven Professional Building located near the courthouse downtown.

"This new office," said George Franks, "will enable us to increase both our staff and the range of services provided." In addition, the location is easily accessible by public transportation.

Franks, who first began his practice in Pasadena on King Street in 1980 with a staff of two, now employs a staff of 12, including four junior partners and full-time editor/production coordinator. The new office, located on the second floor of the Professional Building, occupies 3,600 square feet.

Franks said, "In the last year and a half it became apparent that our old office had simply become too small and that we could not provide the level of service our clients were accustomed to." Franks is a member of the California State Society of Architects and the American Institute of Architecture.

Your release, if used, is printed based on the newspaper's needs, availability of space, prominence of you and your firm, and a host of other factors already at play. Any contact that you attempt to make after submitting a release is usually perceived as an irritation to the editor. "So write'm, send'm, and relax!"

PUBLIC "THANK-YOU" MESSAGES

Another way to generate publicity is through a public "thank you" message. This method has been used successfully many times. It is not perceived as an advertisement (although you must pay for it similarly to paid advertising). The objective is to draw attention to your firm by showing appreciation for your clients.

The way to do this is to place an ad, usually in the local news or business section of the newspaper, stating that your firm "wishes to thank its 250 (or whatever number you wish!) clients for letting us help you with your hopes and dreams. May your coming years be as profitable as the ones that have passed." Variations of this message will also be effective. You then list the name, address, and telephone number of your firm. This message has been known to bring in many calls, and because it does not appear to be advertising, you maintain a low-key, professional image. A sample is presented in Exhibit 32.

EXHIBIT 32   SAMPLE PUBLIC THANK YOU NOTICE

Ronald Smith and Company
Consulting Engineers
Lexington
Wishes its 250 clients a very
Merry Christmas. Thanks
for sharing your
dreams with us.
May next year
be your best.

LETTERS TO THE EDITOR

Have you ever considered sending a letter to the editor? As a business professional you certainly have something of merit to say regarding issues that affect your community. Why not say it on the editorial page?

Some guidelines for submitting letters to the editor are presented in Exhibit 33.

EXHIBIT 33   SUBMITTING LETTERS TO THE EDITOR

Type your letter, keeping it short and to the point

Include your name, affiliation, address, and all telephone numbers (the editor may call you to verify that it was in fact you who sent the letter, or to obtain clarification)

Provide the editor with a title or prelude to your letter, i.e., "In Response to Your Article on XYZ . . ." or "On the Issue of UVW . . ."

Avoid accusative, rhetorical, or cynical overtones

Suggest a solution, if possible, to the issue or problem to which you have alluded

Your local press needs you as much as you need them. The successful professional actively uses the press to promote his/her firm.

In Chapter 17, we examine the use of advertising—a most expensive marketing tool.

ADVERTISING

ADVERTISING HAS traditionally been defined as any paid form of nonpersonal presentation of ideas, goods, or services by an identified sponsor. Advertising can involve the use of a wide variety of media, including magazines and newspapers; outdoor posters; signs; novelties, including calendars, desk blotters, and the like; direct mail; and publications such as catalogs, directories, circulars, bulletins, brochures and pamphlets—to name but a few.

In this chapter, we'll focus on the following questions:

- ☐ What are some of the objectives of advertising?
- ☐ What type of information should be included in an effective professional service firm advertisement?
- ☐ Why is it difficult for a small firm to effectively establish an advertising budget?
- ☐ If you hire an individual or agency to assist with your advertising plans, what are some of the control techniques that you should adopt?

☐   What are some techniques for stretching your advertising dollar?

THE OBJECTIVES OF ADVERTISING

Advertising as it relates specifically to professional services is the use of direct mail and advertisements in magazines and newspapers to present both informative and persuasive communications that are designed for and targeted to present clients, potential clients, and all other public groups or individuals who you have decided you would like to reach and influence.

E. Jerome McCarthy, in *Basic Marketing—a Managerial Approach*, says that "every advertisement and every advertising campaign should be seeking clearly defined objectives." He lists basic advertising objectives, some of which any individual advertiser would logically be seeking. Here is an adapted version of McCarthy's list for use by professional service firms:

1.   Aid in the introduction of new services to specific targets.
2.   Assist in the expansion or maintenance of an identified market.
3.   Enhance the firm's personal selling efforts. (Move a target from one stage of the buying process to the next.)
4.   Keep your firm's name before targets.
5.   Provide information regarding the availability of new services and possible application of other services.
6.   Provide contact with identified targets when personal selling cannot be undertaken.
7.   Aid in the establishment of the firm's image.
8.   Induce the target market to take swift action (i.e., get in touch with your firm).
9.   Help clients to confirm their decision to hire your firm.

A properly executed advertising campaign can potentially affect the profitability of your firm. It can also round out your total marketing program. Similar to other tools, however, it cannot in itself substitute for provision of excellent services, sell the services per se, or create and maintain relationships.

WHAT TO ADVERTISE

In a survey recently conducted it was learned that business professionals believe advertising will make the public more aware of the availability of services, and advertising can be tastefully used.

The information that can be effectively advertised includes:

Availability of services.

Specialization in certain areas of the profession.

Specialization in certain industries.

Date firm was established.

Announcement of changes in personnel, location, or hours.

HOW MUCH TO SPEND?

The hallmark of an effective advertising program is to prepare a budget well in advance of actual expenditures. Historically, advertising expenditures have equaled approximately one percent of total revenues for professional services, based on Troy's *Almanac of Business and Industrial Financial Ratios*. Thus a firm receiving $1,000,000 in annual revenue could be expected to spend approximately $10,000 per year on advertising. Advertising in newspapers and business periodicals can be very expensive, however, and the smaller firm may find the cost to be prohibitive.

Focusing on a hypothetical firm with revenues of $1,000,000 per year and an advertising budget of $10,000, the task of allocating that $10,000 (or other amount if so chosen) soon becomes tricky. Decisions must be made regarding Yellow Pages advertising, brochures, and business cards, as well as directory listings and miscellaneous printed materials to accompany mailings.

Malcolm Barnes, a Washington, DC-based graphic arts and advertising consultant, denotes that it is difficult to advise professional service firms on how much to spend for the creation of an effective advertising program. For an established firm, an effective brochure and statement of qualifications is a must. For the younger firm whose personnel, qualifications, and even address is constantly changing, this can turn into a major project.

Initially, a business needs more advertising to gain recognition. Regardless of the age of the firm, the decision to establish an ongoing advertising and promotion budget must be based on realistic projections of anticipated annual gross sales.

THREE WAYS TO SPEND ON ADVERTISING

Three methods of determining an advertising budget are:

1. *Percent of Sales Method.* Stable firms often take the previous year's sales figure as a base for the upcoming year's advertising budget. The advantage of this method is that it is traditional and convenient and also subject to quick review in light of sales gains or decreases. However, this method looks backward and may perpetuate last year's mistakes. This method also tends to overlook increased costs of media and production.

2. *Task Method.* This is based on concrete estimates of the job to be done. The firm sets a specific goal and then spends when and where needed to achieve that goal with every dollar at their command. This assumes confident, responsible, and imaginative management of the entire marketing plan and also involves constant awareness of advertising themes and trends and what the competition is doing. Most budgets are based on a mix of percentage of sales and task method.

3. *Empirical Method.* This method assumes that the way to determine the optimum to spend on advertising is to actually run a series of tests at different levels of advertising. This method requires detailed planning, patience, and a large budget for testing. It also requires discipline in not drawing hasty conclusions.

As one might readily determine, none of the three traditional methods of budgeting successfully provides the small firm with a clear indication of how much to spend on advertising.

SEEK OUTSIDE HELP

To maintain a consistent advertising and promotion program with effective follow-up, it might be necessary to hire a parttime creative person or to employ an agency to perform similar tasks. It is best to avoid the do-it-yourself approach to advertising.

Working with an advertising agency basically requires the gradual building of a relationship. Trust is built over time through continuing and open communication. This begins when you work on your first advertising campaign together. At this time, you will need to come to agreement on:

1. *Objectives.* What do you want to accomplish?
2. *Market.* Whom do you wish to reach?
3. *Message.* What do you wish to convey?
4. *Media.* Which media will be used?
5. *Evaluation.* How will the results be evaluated?

Here are some tips from Barnes for building and maintaining an effective relationship with an agency or freelancer:

1. Hire only those with experience in the primary media in which you intend to advertise (i.e., the local newspaper).

2. Show and use your knowledge of advertising techniques when directing the firm or individual you hired to help discourage misuse of funds or overspending.

3. Seek an individual or firm that has handled similar accounts and has good media contacts, including editors, writers, graphic artists, photographers, and typesetters.

4. Always ask for a copy of any ad that is run. This will serve as a double check against late publications, poor-quality results, and mistakes.

5. Create an advertising file to include masters of all ads run, a copy of the actual publication, and an invoice for all expenses incurred. This will help greatly in adjusting the budget for current spending and in projecting for the next year.

STRETCHING YOUR ADVERTISING DOLLARS

To stretch your advertising dollars, consider these suggestions:

1. *Seek Complementary Advertising.* If an advertisement of yours says "located next to Brown's Hardware," make sure that Brown says he is located next to you in his advertisements.

2. *Seek Exchange of Services.*   If a local editor needs your services, you might barter for an ad or two in that editor's publication.

3. *Check with Your Professional Trade Association.*   Consult them to see if they offer assistance through standard industry copy, formats, logos, and the like.

For the small professional service firm, the effective use of advertising—in light of cost, time, and effort required—may prove to be an inordinate task. Through the use of the other nonpersonal promotion tools discussed, even a small firm can establish a system that effectively places the name of the firm in front of appropriate targets at a reasonable cost.

Chapter 18 focuses on brochures, regarded by many as indispensable.

18

BROCHURES

A BROCHURE serves as a central source of printed information to existing and potential clients. Although there are no absolutes about what the brochure should contain, most experts agree that an effective brochure contains information on your firm's (1) history, (2) philosophy, (3) organizational structure, and (4) service areas. Your brochure should enhance your image as it literally represents you on paper. It should also be designed to project uniqueness—to make you and your firm stand out from all of your competitors.

In this chapter we'll help you to answer the following questions:

☐ Keeping in mind the need to produce a client-centered brochure, what type of information do prospective clients want to gain from your brochure?

☐ What is a quick way to determine which type of brochure is right for you?

☐ Should you attempt to complete your brochure in-house?

☐ What are some of the design options available in the development of your brochures?

157

NOT AN EASY JOB

Production of your firm's brochure is a complex undertaking and one that requires significant effort. Exhibit 34 illustrates 14 brochure formats including the standard format (see format 9). For most professional service firms, it is desirable to lay the groundwork for the development of the brochure but ultimately rely on outside assistance for completion. In undertaking this project, you may ask yourself (1) what target you wish to reach and (2) what message you wish to offer.

A CLIENT-CENTERED BROCHURE

Most professionals as well as other business entrepreneurs end up producing a brochure that perhaps supplies ego gratification but does

EXHIBIT 34   BROCHURE FORMATS

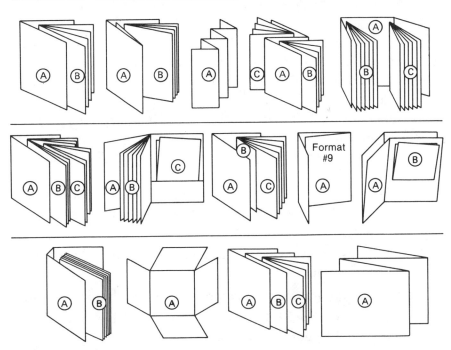

not adhere to the needs of the client and hence does not follow the client-centered approach. *Your brochure is not for you, it is for your clients and prospective clients, and should be developed for their needs.*

Your firm's brochure, in the words of Ted Eisenberg, president of Ted Eisenberg Associates, "is, in effect, an expensive, illustrated calling card."

A prospective client will certainly be interested in the basic information about your firm, including history, philosophy, organization, structure, and service areas. Specifically, however, the client will also be interested in learning about:

1. The qualifications of your staff.

2. The quality of your service.

3. The size and location of your offices.

4. The range of your services.

5. Your firm's reputation.

6. Your firm's experience in specific industries.

7. Others who have used your services.

8. How long you've been in business.

For the small practitioner with little change in personnel, it is permissible to include pictures, a short biography, and other references to yourself or staff personnel. For slightly larger firms, this may be a costly mistake as personnel turnover, the addition of new partners, or other developments render the brochure outdated. To alleviate this problem, you might try producing separate flaps describing individual staff that can be inserted into jackets within the main section of the brochure.

SCANNING THE COMPETITION

A quick way to determine what type of brochure will be right for you is to assemble the brochures of competitors and study their efforts. If your collection is not large, this would be a good time to write for and acquire the brochures of others so that you can more properly undertake this exercise. Writing to firms outside your trade area will probably yield better results than writing to those firms that are direct competitors.

After you've assembled at least ten brochures of other firms, carefully review those features that appeal to you. There are hundreds of factors to consider. The following list represents a mere subset of all the options available in developing your brochure:

Use of flaps, pockets, foldovers	Use of color
Dimensions of brochure	Use of testimonials
Quality of paper	Use of bulleted sections
Use of pictures	Action photographs
Weight (affects mailing cost)	Spacing
Staff biographies	Heading, titles
Client lists	Captions
Sketches	Style of print
Number of pages	Association affiliations

CONSULT A SPECIALIST

You will eventually need to turn over the development of your brochure to a marketing or graphics specialist. The key to effective use of an outside resource is to produce a rough prototype of your desired end product. Sketch out on several pieces of paper the layout and content of each brochure page. If your photographs are to be enclosed, leave space accordingly.

In the selection of outside assistance, try to seek marketing or advertising professionals who have experience working with firms similar to yours and ask to see samples of their work. Refer back to the discussion on using a graphics specialist in Chapter 17, for this certainly applies in the development of your brochure.

The cost of your brochure can range anywhere from $1,000 to $2,000 per page, and it is the number of pages—not the number of brochure copies printed—that is the single biggest cost factor. The proper size or number of pages is a trade-off between your budget and what is needed to deliver your message effectively. (*Note*: A single sheet with material printed on both sides counts as two pages.)

An effective brochure works hard at marketing and promoting your firm. Thus the dollars invested in producing a high-quality product can be dollars well spent.

Chapter 19, on other promotional tools, rounds out Part 3 on nonpersonal promotion.

19

OTHER PROMOTIONAL TOOLS

BUSINESS CARDS and other promotional tools and sundries help to place or keep your firm's name in front of targets of opportunity and influence. In this chapter we discuss the development and use of these items and their significance in your overall marketing and promotional effort. After reading this chapter you should be able to answer these questions:

☐   Can business cards alone bring in clients?

☐   What are some of the physical characteristics of professionally developed business cards?

☐   In what types of directory can your firm be listed?

☐   What are some ways to maintain good public relations?

☐   Can use of promotional sundries bring in clients?

BUSINESS CARDS SUPPORT YOUR EFFORTS

The fact that you have business cards is not likely to bring any clients in the door; however, business cards support your overall marketing and promotion efforts and will certainly serve as a reminder to those who are favorably influenced toward you and most likely to contact you. An impressive business card is shown in Exhibit 35.

A quick and effective way to develop a business card that is consistent with your desired image and provides fundamental information to your targets is to assemble and examine all business cards of other professionals, particularly those in your field, in a manner similar to what you did in Chapter 18.

You will probably notice that most cards are either white, light beige, or very light yellow or gold and conform to the 3.5-inch by 2-inch norm. Although there are no hard-and-fast rules about what makes for an effective, attractive business card, the following elements appear to be of significance:

1.   The corporate logo is strategically placed on the card.

2.   Often the name of the firm is set off from other information, has a different style of print, and is unusually colored (possibly gold or blue).

EXHIBIT 35   A MOST UNUSUAL BUSINESS CARD (reduced 46.7%)

3. The title and middle initial of the card bearer are included.

4. The information contained on the card is balanced and does not necessarily emphasize any particular information item.

5. Supporting descriptive information is generally absent from established or conservatively imaged firms.

6. The name of the individual is in slightly larger print than other information such as address or phone number.

7. There's an absence of garish colors.

8. Textured paper with embossed lettering is often used.

9. Printing is contained on only one side of the card.

10. Black, dark gray, or dark blue print appear to be most authoritative.

CARE AND TREATMENT OF BUSINESS CARDS

In addition to the preceding observations, the following tips will be helpful in the care and treatment of your business cards:

1. Discard dog-eared cards because they indicate that they've been in your wallet for an extended period of time.

2. Avoid writing additional messages on the card if possible; if necessary, have new cards produced rather than "use up" outdated cards.

3. Avoid using cards as scratch paper, particularly in the presence of prospective clients.

The cost for, say, 500 business cards varies widely. Many mail order stationery firms offer deals such as 500 standard-size cards, white paper, blue printing at a cost of $10 to $12. Cards that bear your unique logo, are embossed, and are ingrained off white paper will be several times more expensive. Cards may be ordered through office supply stores, printers, copy centers, and gift shops.

PROMOTIONAL TOOLS

Many professionals overlook the fact that they can obtain a directory listing for free or a very small fee by creatively seeking various printing sources in their area. For example, in metropolitan areas where the telephone directories are larger than an inch thick, you will often see a community telephone directory consisting of local merchants. Chances are that placing a display advertisement or one-line listing may bring in additional business.

Other places where your firm may be listed include Chamber of Commerce directories, neighborhood telephone directories, community business guides, merchant desk blotters, minority business directories, shopping center guides, local Small Business Administration circulars, and other privately published directories of business and professional services. Your local librarian can quickly identify numerous directory sources of interest.

Other publicity generators may be effective, depending on your situation:

1. *Offer Free Meeting Room.* If you have the room within your offices, you may consider offering free meeting space to local civic organizations or charities. Such groups may require space for as little as a few hours one night a month. This is an excellent way to build a good community image and generate publicity about your firm.

2. *Run for Public Office.* Much publicity and community recognition can be gained by running for a noncontroversial public office. Granted, funds will have to be spent to develop and distribute campaign literature, but win or lose, you stand to gain broad exposure within the community. Although it may appear time-consuming to seek public office, it's a fast way to achieve community recognition.

3. *Volunteer to Appear on Local Radio and TV Programs.* Although few business professionals recognize this extremely valuable publicity vehicle, local radio and television stations often

are in desperate need of guests for their community-oriented programming. By volunteering to serve as a guest and discuss areas of interest to the viewing or listening public, you can gain instant local recognition.*

4. *Offer a Community "Good Citizen" Award.* Each week or month, have someone on your clerical staff scan local newspapers and publications to find stories on individuals who have performed some good deed for the community. As you select each week's or month's winner, send an award or certificate to the individual with a letter explaining your program. Duplicate letters should then be sent to local media who may wish to report on your award system. If space allows, display the names of winners within your office. This will draw interest among people who see it. In the long run, maintenance of this award system will generate very effective community relations and publicity.

5. *Send Congratulatory Notes.* A good way of gaining favor with targets is to write congratulatory notes to those who have been cited for various honors. You might assign a clerical person to read newspapers and magazines and establish a clip file to enable you to continuously send notes to appropriate targets.

PROMOTIONAL SUNDRIES

Other minor items that have been used by professionals in support of the overall marketing and promotional effort include calendars, rulers, note pads, tax calendars, pens, pencils, plastic folders, and other novelties. The significance and degree to which a measurable impact on marketing is facilitated through the use of these items is not clear.

For the smaller firm, depending on the local business environ-

*Robert Freda, a principal with Golden, Freda & Schraub, P. C. of Washington, DC called a local radio station to which he frequently listens, and volunteered to speak on the topic of wills. In just two days he was invited to be a guest on the station and as a result received a couple of new clients who needed wills.

ment, the type of client served, and the desired image, these items may be perfectly acceptable for distribution. Other firms may regard these items as superfluous or marginally effective marketing tools and choose to ignore their use completely.

The decision to use promotional sundries is essentially up to you. There are, however, no penalties that are readily apparent from not using them.

You've now completed Part 3 and are ready to put your client-centered marketing approach into strategic focus.

PART

4

STRATEGIC FOCUS AND YOUR MARKETING PLAN

THIS BOOK has concentrated on the development of a client-centered approach to marketing your professional and consulting services. By now you should have absorbed the principles of client-centered marketing. It's still relatively easy to skip back or fall into old habits, though, especially when marketing your services.

Failure to embrace the client-centered marketing approach inevitably leads to one of the common marketing mistakes:

Defining and Limiting Marketing to "Getting New Clients." This is a most frequent and troublesome mistake. This action has the unintended effects of (1) "turning off" staff—who wish that marketing would go away—and (2) neglecting present engagements, which can serve as major needs identification tools offering opportunities to sense, serve, and satisfy the needs of a virtually "captive" market at minimum expense and at minimum risk of personal rejection. Consider the CPA who defined marketing as "getting new clients" and was quite successful at obtaining new clients. Inadvertently the accountant neglected to work at retaining sound relationships with his better clients and found that referrals dropped off. He was required to re-bid annual audit engagements and thus face "buy-in" strategies on the part of large national firms that had excess capacity and were willing to price their services at a discount.

Becoming Obsessed with Growth for Growth's Sake. This plagues many firms. If the firm is not careful, it may trade "class for mass." The unintended results of this obsession include (1) "operation scramble" as a way of life because the volume of work and nature of the assignments leads to scheduling, staffing, and engagement problems, (2) reduction in net income because much time and funds are dedicated to obtaining new clients, and finally (3) difficulty in differentiating your services and client focus from those of other firms.

Attempting to be "All Good Things" to All Types of Clients. This marketing strategy is also fraught with problems. In this era of specialization and concentration, marketing leadership and profit result from being seen as "somebody special to some special bodies." Unless you pass the "D&B test," which means that your services are perceived as being different and/or better than others, you face increased price sensitivity by clients and prospective clients.

How, then, do the client-centered marketers maintain proper orientation and strategic focus on the most lucrative and professionally rewarding markets or niches in which to provide their services? Moreover, what questions do strategic managers ask in maintaining a client-centered marketing approach?

Read on.

20

DEVELOPING A STRATEGIC FOCUS

A NEW era for professional service firms commenced in January 1982. The U.S. Supreme Court issued a new ruling that is expected to have profound impact on the management and marketing of professional services. The court struck down tight restrictions on advertising by lawyers, thereby freeing all the professions "for promotional campaigns more comparable to ordinary business advertising."

This chapter will help you to answer the following questions:

☐ Why is the strategic management of marketing a challenge for most professionals?

☐ How does the strategic thinker regard the "status quo"?

☐ Does the strategic thinker concentrate more on increased volume or increasing profitability?

☐ How can an insider's view of the niche be developed?

A HISTORIC RULING FOR PROFESSIONAL SERVICES

Back in 1977 the U.S. Supreme Court reached a decision that lifted what had been an absolute prohibition on lawyer advertising. Thus from 1977 to only recently, law firms were allowed to advertise as long as descriptions of their specialties were confined to predetermined categories. For example, a lawyer who handled divorces and separations could self-advertise as a practitioner of "family law." With the new ruling, the terms "divorce" or "separation" may now be used in paid advertisements. Similarly, all other professionals apparently are free to use more precise terminology when advertising and promoting their services as long as all claims are accurate.

STRATEGIC MANAGEMENT OF MARKETING

Strategic actions relate to the nature and direction of a practice. The fundamental strategic action is to decide whom one will serve and in what ways. The survival and prosperity of all but the largest "full-service" firms will, in large measure, depend on finding a niche or niches. The key will be to develop and promote client-centered services that fill the unmet (or poorly met) needs of clients and targeted prospective clients in their niche(s).

PROFILE OF THE STRATEGIC THINKER

The strategic management of marketing and the development of a strategic thought process is, indeed, a challenge for most service professionals because they lack education and experience in this area. Let's profile the strategic thinker by examining the types of questions asked and other factors:

1. The strategic thinker develops a client-centered orientation. The client's needs represent a starting point from which marketing

strategy is based. The strategic thinker knows that learning what the client values and expects is fundamental to sustaining a profitable practice. In short, the strategic thinker is client driven.

2. The strategic thinker puts the status quo on trial and asks pointed questions such as: "Where are we now? Where are we going? Where do we wish to be going? What will we look like when we get there?" As simple as these questions may seem, few successful professionals have posed them; however, the answers to these questions are important in the strategic management of the practice.

3. The strategic thinker is able to identify strengths and match them with present and potential market opportunities. As Peter Drucker opines, he "feeds opportunities and starves problems." The strategic manager takes the steps necessary to capitalize on high payoff opportunities. Conversely, sacred cows and unprofitable practice areas must be abandoned without passion.

4. The strategic thinker is able to focus on profitability and not necessarily volume, with the goal of working fewer hours but at an increasingly higher hourly rate. This person is also alert to opportunities to employ greater leverage using junior staff personnel but does not make the mistake of trading "class for mass" —a well-developed base of "high-class," prompt-paying clients is desirable over dealing with the multitudes.

MANAGING YOUR MARKETING STRATEGICALLY

Marketing information is a valuable resource in directing a professional practice toward its most profitable marketing mix. Many firms are beginning to realize the importance of accumulating client and market data, and after analysis, basing their marketing actions on the results.

The successful, profitable professional service firm of the 1980s and 1990s will have identified its niche(s). The nature of existing client relationships and growth potential in the industry, as well as the skills, reputation, and interest of the professional will, of course, play a major role in the identification of the niche(s).

The development of a client-centered or insider's understanding of the niche must be developed. This can be done by maintaining an overview of the trends and problems of the niche on a continuous basis. What are the needs of the niche, who is buying, how much are they buying, and what do they value? Contact must be made with targets of influence (see Chapter 7) that ultimately may serve as referral sources. The key to maintaining understanding is to always be able to readily relate experiences of the firm in dealing with and serving the needs of the niche.

IF NECESSARY, REORGANIZE THE FIRM

The successful professional recognizes the need to organize or reorganize the practice to serve the niche most effectively. This may require the appointment or addition of a partner who will coordinate activities, monitor trends, and manage the services to meet the expectations of clients and prospective clients. The designated partner should also be responsible for providing any staff training in marketing and utilizing existing engagements to identify additional client needs.

The successful professional must work to develop an insider's reputation with the niche or target market. Clients must feel that the services you provide are uniquely tailored to their needs and that the existence of your practice within a convenient distance represents "provident proximity." The goal in developing an insider's reputation with the niche is to be viewed as "somebody special to some special bodies."

The professions are in a new era that is characterized by rapid and radical changes. The application of strategic management to client-centered marketing will carry professionals through this era and ensure survival and prosperity.

Now let's put the pieces together for preparation of your marketing plan.

21

PREPARING YOUR MARKETING PLAN

YOU HAVE now been thoroughly immersed in the client-centered marketing approach for the marketing of your professional and consulting services.

It's now time to organize and coordinate those activities that will develop and enhance your relationship with those people who will be interested in using, retaining, or referring to others your firm and your services. This is most efficiently done by preparing a marketing plan. The charts and worksheets used throughout the book, added to your research efforts and scheduling of client-centered marketing activities, comprise a sound marketing plan.

This chapter assists you in preparing your market plan and also provides answers to the following questions:

☐   What are the components of a client-centered marketing plan?

☐   Must some marketing related thinking occur each day?

☐   Will an effectively implemented client-centered marketing plan work for you?

A CLIENT-CENTERED MARKETING PLAN

A client-centered marketing plan for a professional service firm consists of five components:

1. Auditing one's practice and markets to identify opportunities and problems.
2. Establishing priority.
3. Setting goals to be accomplished during the marketing planning period.
4. Allocating and organizing the resources required to accomplish the period's goals.
5. Scheduling, applying, and monitoring results.

The end product or "hard-copy" is the marketing plan.

Market planning converts your intentions into commitment and your insights into action. *You must put your plan in writing.*

On completion of a training workshop in setting marketing goals, one firm decided to use their copier to reduce the written plan to pocket size, laminate it, and offer it to staff professionals as a daily memory jogger.

Putting your ideas in writing provides discipline. Hazy thoughts can become precisely formulated strategies when committed to writing. A written plan enables you to measure your progress and to experience a satisfying feeling of accomplishment as you note completion dates for each part of your plan.

Blank forms of all the exhibits discussed throughout the book that comprise your plan have been reprinted in Appendix C for easy copying. You may wish to modify some charts for your own specific needs. In preparing your plan, keep it simple. As a general rule, when in doubt, leave it out. Minimize the use of any additional forms and record keeping, and you'll minimize the time needed to do a good job in individual marketing.

Attempt some marketing related thinking or action daily. Your objective is to make marketing a habitual action and thought pattern.

SELECT LITTLE GOALS TO START

During your initial marketing planning sessions, select goals that can be worked on a piecemeal basis. For example, complete Exhibit 7a by the week of __/ /__. Establish a schedule for the completion of all other charts in a similar manner.

To aid in initiating the marketing planning process, we provide sample goal statements in Exhibit 36, sample financial goals statements in Exhibit 37, and a refresher list of client-centered marketing activities in Exhibit 38.

EXHIBIT 36   SAMPLE GOAL STATEMENTS

Performance

Financial

Increase average chargeable hour rate from $_____ to $_____ by __/__.
Bill __ hours in month of _____.
Identify delinquent accounts by __/__.

Existing Clients

Identify causes of lost clients by __/__.
Contact _____ at _____ to discuss _____ by __/__.

Existing Markets

Identify existing markets by __/__.
Select one market to estimate potential for growth by __/__.

Existing Services

Assess client-centeredness of $\underset{\text{(service)}}{_____}$ by __/__.

Assess payoff from specialization in $\underset{\text{(industry)}}{_____}$ by __/__.

Referrals

Assess the quality of relationship with $\underset{\text{(who)}}{_____}$ by __/__.

Select one referral to "educate" about $\underset{\text{(what)}}{_____}$ by __/__.

Targets

Select one prospective client in potential new business pipeline for follow-up sales contact by __/__.
Identify desirable potential clients in industry _____ by __/__.

Promotion

Establish promotion objectives by __/__.
Schedule entertainment with $\underset{\text{(client)}}{_____}$ by __/__.

Other

Attend $\underset{\text{(program)}}{_____}$ on __/__.

Read $\underset{\text{(publication)}}{_____}$ by __/__.

180

EXHIBIT 37 SAMPLE FINANCIAL GOALS STATEMENTS

For: _____, (__/__/__) to (__/__/__)

My financial goals for this period are: _____

_____

I intend to increase my personal billing revenue from _____
(most recent 12 months)

to $_____, an increase of __%.

I intend to increase the number of personal chargeable hours from __ to __,

an increase/decrease of __%.

I want/intend to increase my average *hourly rate* from $__ to $__.

My key goal to accomplish in this period is: _____

_____

_____

During this planning period I also intend to accomplish the following: _____

_____

_____

The problems I anticipate, if any, in achieving these goals are:_____

_____

_____

The resources I can draw on to help me overcome these problems include:

_____

_____
_____

EXHIBIT 38 CLIENT-CENTERED MARKETING ACTIVITY—
A REFRESHER

Existing Key Clients

Retention planning for _____
Expanding services for _____
Referral development with _____

Existing Marginal Clients

Upgrade service and financial relationships with _____
Terminate or transfer _____

Other Existing Client Actions

Corrective actions to remove causes of lost clients _____
Actions to capitalize on sources of desirable new clients _____
Other _____

Markets and Niches

To research _____
To penetrate _____
To abandon _____

Referral Sources

Improve relationships with _____
Develop additional sources—leverage _____
Contact to educate _____

Build in follow-up. When you set an accomplishment date for a goal, note this in your pocket calendar and desk calendar as a reminder. If you constantly miss goals, determine why. Remember, results accrue over a period of time.

The client-centered marketing approach has proved successful for professional service firms, from some of the very largest to one-person firms.

If you effectively implement your client-centered marketing plan, it will work for you.

GLOSSARY

ACTION LETTER   A management letter that enhances the professional-client relationship by displaying the same level of quality as the rest of your professional services.

ADVERTISING   Any paid form of nonpersonal presentation of ideas, goods, or services by an identified sponsor. Can involve the use of any form of media.

ATMOSPHERICS   That part of your personal image that is reflected by your office decor, location, staffing, and layout.

BULK RATE   A reduced rate offered by the U.S. Post Office for mass mailers.

CLIENT-CENTERED MARKETING   The continuing process of developing and enhancing relationships with receptive people who are or can be useful to you in using, retaining, and referring you and your services.

COST PER THOUSAND   The price a list compiler charges for on-time use of mailing labels of a specified target group.

DIRECT MAIL   A form of advertising in which a business communication is sent to preselected targets.

EXISTING CLIENT   A client you now serve or will serve during the coming period.

GOAL   A specific statement of what you expect or intend to accomplish and when.

HARD-SELL APPROACH   A marketing approach that focuses on getting known, and places emphasis on "our firm" and "our services" but does not focus on client needs.

IMAGE   The sum total of all the perceptions your clients and all others have about you and your practice.

KEY, "A" CLIENT   A client whom you consider to be of exceptional value to you because of fee volume, prestige, potential for growth, and so on.

LEVERAGING   The process of identifying and capitalizing on the smallest number of actions that produce the greatest results.

LIST COMPILER/SUPPLIER   A direct mail marketing organization that provides names and addresses of target markets for a fee.

LOGO   A symbol or design (used on stationery and literature) that aids others in identifying and remembering you, your firm, or your organization.

MARGINAL CLIENT   A client whom you consider to be a problem because of fees, collection difficulty, or practices you can't support.

MARKET   All your existing, prospective, and potential clients in an industry and those influentials such as association executives and editors. Your market is an "arena" where buying and selling occurs.

MARKETING PLAN   The "hard-copy" end-product of the Marketing Planning Process.

MARKETING PLANNING   The continuing process of: (1) auditing one's practice and markets to identify opportunities and problems, (2) establishing priority, (3) setting goals, (4) allocating and organizing resources required to accomplish the goals, and (5) scheduling, doing, and monitoring results.

NEWS RELEASE   An announcement of community, state, national or international interest distributed to print media by the organization for whom the release is about.

NICHE   A target market or industry segment within which you can readily and prosperously serve.

PERSONAL PROMOTION   First person activities that you undertake to favorably present your capabilities in meeting client needs.

PERSONAL SELLING   A professional marketing effort involving face-to-face communication and feedback with prospective users and influences of your services.

PRESS RELEASE   See "News Release" above.

PRIMARY MARKETS   A target group or industry that constitutes a relatively large percentage of your total revenue.

PROMOTION   The process of informing, persuading, or reminding targets of opportunity and influence about your firm's ability to meet client needs. Also involves stimulating inquiries and managing your image.

PROPOSAL   A document that is designed to describe the firm's ability to perform a specific task (or tasks). Indicates that the firm has the facilities, human resources, management experience, and track record to assure successful project performance and completion.

PROSPECTING   The task of securing appointments with targets or nonclients who may have need for your services.

PUBLIC RELATIONS   All planned activities that you undertake to influence public opinion about you and your firm.

PUBLICITY   A key component of public relations; involves media coverage of events including background information, descriptions, relevant data, or other current information involving you, your service, and your firm or organization.

READERSHIP (OR AUDIENCE) PROFILE   Descriptive information and facts about subscribers (or audience) of media sources.

REFERRALS   Clients and nonclients who mention your name to others and provide you with introductions and leads to new business opportunities.

REPUTATION   The perception of value and integrity that you've demonstrated in serving your clients and community.

RFP   A request for proposal is a solicitation made by a government or private agency that is seeking the services of an outside contractor to perform a specific task or tasks.

STRATEGIC FOCUS   Selecting whom one will serve and in what ways, then developing and promoting services that fill unmet or poorly met needs of clients and prospective clients.

STRATEGIC THINKER   In the context of marketing professional services one who develops a client-centered orientation, identifies strengths and matches them with present potential market opportunities, and focuses on profitability, not necessarily volume. The strategic thinker puts the status quo on trial and asks pointed questions.

TARGETS OF INFLUENCE   Nonclient referral sources who, while not likely to use your services, may favorably influence others to do so.

TARGETS OF OPPORTUNITY   Organizations, firms, and individuals that may have need for your services and who represent service/revenue opportunities for your firm.

TRADITIONAL APPROACH   A marketing approach that is reactive and deals with existing client problems as they arise, but provides little overall strategy or coordination of marketing effort.

UNSOLICITED PROPOSAL   A proposal written in response to a perceived or known need and not in response to an RFP.

FURTHER READING

BOOKS

Becker, Franklin, *The Successful Office*, Addison Wesley, Reading, MA, 1982.

Belkin, Gary S., *Getting Published*, John Wiley & Sons, New York, 1984.

Carnegie, Dale, *The Quick and Easy Way to Effective Speaking*, Association Press, New York, 1976.

Cox, Weld, *Marketing Architectural and Engineering Services*, Van Nostrand Reinhold, New York, 1980.

Denney, Robert W., *Marketing Accounting Services*, Van Nostrand Reinhold, New York, 1983.

Hensley, Dennis E., *Become Famous, Then Rich: How to Promote Yourself and Your Business*, R & R Newkirk, Indianapolis, 1983.

Jeffries, James R. and Bates, Jefferson D., *The Executive's Guide to Meetings, Conferences & Audiovisual Presentations*, McGraw Hill Book Company, New York, 1983.

Knesel, Dave, *Free Publicity: A Step by Step Guide*, Sterling Publishing Co., New York, 1983.

Kotler, Philip, *Market Management: Analysis Planning and Control*, Prentice-Hall, Englewood Cliffs, NJ, 1980.

Mahon, James J., *The Marketing of Professional Accounting Services: A Personal Practice Development Approach*, 2nd ed., John Wiley & Sons, New York, 1982.

McCarthy, E. Jerome, *Basic Marketing—A Managerial Approach*, 6th ed., Irwin, Homewood, IL, 1978.

Rachlin, Norman S., *Eleven Steps to Building a Profitable Accounting Practice*, McGraw-Hill, New York, 1983.

Rathmell, J. M., Ed., *Marketing in the Service Sector*, Winthrop Publishers, Cambridge, MA, 1974.

Webster, Frederick E., Jr., *Industrial Marketing Strategy*, John Wiley & Sons, New York, 1979.

Wheatley, Edward W., *Marketing Professional Services*, Prentice-Hall, Englewood Cliffs, NJ, 1983.

Wilson, Aubrey, *The Marketing of Professional Services*, McGraw-Hill, New York, 1972.

ARTICLES

Argall Stover, Beryl C., "Firm Brochures and Client Newsletters," *The Practical Accountant*, July 1981, pp. 30–33.

Churchman, Deborah, "A Few Pointers on Weeding Your Overstuffed Calendar," *Christian Science Monitor*, May 17, 1984.

Connor, Richard A., Jr., "Mining The Gold In Your Own Backyard," *The Practicing CPA*, April 1980, pp. 4–5.

Connor, Richard A., Jr., "Client-Centered Marketing: A Survival Strategy," *The Practicing CPA*, April 1981, pp. 6–7.

Connor, Richard A., Jr. and Davidson, Jeffrey P., "Professional Services Consultants Offer Strategies," *The Washington Business Journal*, April 18, 1983, Commentary, p. 3.

Connor, Richard A., Jr. and Davidson, Jeffrey P., "A Little Self-Promotion Can Go a Long Way," *The Commercial Record*, April 13, 1984.

Connor, Richard A., Jr. and Rowe, Gerald R., Jr., "How to Use Your Management Letters to Increase Your Fees," *The Practical Accountant*, January/February 1980.

Connor, Richard A., Jr. and White, J. Larry, "How to Write Client-Centered Management Letters," *C. A. Magazine*, May 1976, pp. 58–60.

Davidson, Jeffrey P., "Tips on Selling to Business and Industry," *Specialty Salesmen*, October 1979, p. 39.

Davidson, Jeffrey P. and Rosenberg, Barry D., "Contract Proposals," *Journal of Applied Management*, July/August 1980.

Davidson, Jeffrey P., "In Praise of Portable Dictation Equipment," *Office*, November 1980.

Davidson, Jeffrey P., "Promoting an Accounting Practice," *The National Public Accountant*, November 1981.

Davidson, Jeffrey P., "The Benefits of Getting Published," *Business Horizons*, March/April 1982.

Davidson, Jeffrey P., "The Three Common Denominators of Sales Success," *Professional Agent*, August 1982.

Davidson, Jeffrey P., "Personal Control is Key to Sales Success," *Selling Direct*, December 1983.

Davidson, Jeffrey P., "Homework in the Office," *Industrial Distribution*, February 1984.

Davidson, Jeffrey P., "Time-Saving Steps for Conducting Research," *Phoenix Business Journal*, April 16, 1984.

Editorial, "Keeping Your Practice Healthy," *American Medical News*, January 30, 1981.

Editorial, "Co-op to Market Traditional Dentistry," *Marketing News*, May 29, 1981, p. 5.

Eisenberg, Ted, "Tips on How to Prepare an Effective Firm Brochure," *The Practical Accountant*, June 1982, pp. 29–32.

George, William R. and Solomon, Paul J., "Marketing Strategies for Improving Practice Development," *The Journal of Accountancy*, February 1980, pp. 79–84.

Goldstein, Daniel A., "Marketing Lawyers' Services in the 1980's," *New York State Bar Journal*, June 1982, p. 202.

Graham, Deborah, "Era of Client Development Has Arrived," *Legal Times*, April 18, 1983, pp. 1, 8.

Gummesson, Evert, "The Marketing of Professional Services—An Organizational Dilemma," *European Journal of Marketing*, May 1979.

Haught, Robert L., "Marketing of Professional Services Gaining Popularity," *Washington Business Review*, June 20, 1983.

Hickman, James R., "A Consultants Primer of Personal Selling," *Journal of Management Consulting*, Fall 1982, p. 38.

Kotler, Philip and Connor, Richard A., Jr., "Marketing Professional Services," *Journal of Marketing*, January 1977.

Maister, David H., "Balancing the Professional Service Firm," *Sloan Management Review*, Fall 1982, p. 15.

Mansfield, Stephanie, "And Today's Features: Screening the Shrinks on Tape," *Washington Post*, October 22, 1982, page C1.

Roth, Roger, "The Blue-Chip Lawyers Discover Marketing," *Business Week*, Special Report, April 25, 1983.

Sogofsky, Irwin, "Marketing Research Firms: Stress Your Strong Suit When Pricing Custom Studies," *Marketing News*, May 14, 1982, p. 1.

Thomsen, Charles, "Marketing is Everybody's Business," *Society for Marketing Professional Services News*, October/November 1982, p. 2.

Warner, Harland W., "A Different Approach: How to Select a Firm," *Public Relations Journal*, October 1983, p. 29.

Welsh, William C., "An Executive's Guide for Getting Into Print," *Management Review*, September 1976, pp. 25–30.

Whisnant, Susan R., Contributing Ed., "Marketing CPA Services," *The CPA Journal*, November 1982 through May 1983.

Wittreich, Warren J., "How To Buy/Sell Professional Services," *Harvard Business Review*, March/April 1966, pp. 127–138.

A SAMPLING OF INDUSTRY, PROFESSIONAL, SMALL BUSINESS, AND TRADE ASSOCIATIONS

ADMINISTRATION, MANAGEMENT

American Management
  Association
135 West 50th Street
New York, NY 10020
(212) 586-8100

American Society for Public
  Administration
1120 G Street, NW, Suite 500
Washington, DC 20005
(202) 393-7878

Data Processing Management
  Association
505 Busse Highway
Park Ridge, IL 60068
(312) 693-5070

National Management
  Association
2210 Arbor Boulevard
Dayton, OH 45439
(513) 294-0421

American Society of Association
Executives
1575 Eye Street, NW
Washington, DC 20005
(202) 626-2723

Sales & Marketing Executives,
International
380 Lexington Avenue
New York, NY 10168
(212) 239-1919

COMMUNICATIONS, GRAPHICS, AND PRINTING

American Association of
Advertising Agencies
666 Third Avenue
New York, NY 10017
(212) 682-2500

Institute for Graphic
Communication, Inc.
375 Commonwealth Avenue
Boston, MA 02115
(617) 267-9425

Direct Mail/Marketing Association
6 East 43rd Street
New York, NY 10017
(212) 689-4977

Printing Industries of America
1730 North Lunn Street
Arlington, VA 22209
(703) 841-8100

International Association of
Business Communicators
870 Market Street, Suite 940
San Francisco, CA 94102
(415) 433-3400

Professional Photographers of
America, Inc.
1090 Executive Way
Des Plaines, IL 60018
(312) 299-8161

International Communications
Association
12750 Merit Drive, Suite 828, LB-89
Dallas, TX 75251
(214) 233-3889

Public Relations Society of
America
845 Third Avenue
New York, NY 10022
(212) 826-1750

CONSTRUCTION, CONTRACTING

Air Conditioning Contractors of
America
1228 17th Street, NW
Washington, DC 20036
(202) 296-7610

National Association of Home
Builders
15th and M Streets, NW
Washington, DC 20005
(202) 822-0200

American Subcontractors
Association
8401 Corporate Drive, Suite 540
Landover, MD 20785
(301) 459-8494

Associated Builders & Contractors,
Inc.
729 15th Street, NW
Washington, DC 20005
(202) 637-8800

Associated General Contractors
of America
1957 E Street, NW
Washington, DC 20006
(202) 393-2040

National Electrical Contractors
Association
7315 Wisconsin Avenue, 13th Floor
Bethesda, MD 20814
(301) 657-3110

National Remodelers Association
11 East 44th Street
New York, NY 10017
(212) 867-0121

Painting and Decorating
Contractors
7223 Lee Highway
Falls Church, VA 22046
(703) 534-1201

FINANCIAL, REAL ESTATE

American Bankers Association
1120 Connecticut Avenue, NW
Washington, DC 20036
(202) 467-4000

American Institute of Real Estate
Appraisers
430 North Michigan Avenue
Chicago, IL 60611
(312) 329-8200

American Society of Appraisers
11800 Sunrise Valley Drive,
Suite 400
Reston, VA 22091
(703) 620-3838

Mortgage Bankers Association of
America
1125 15th Street, NW
Washington, DC 20005
(202) 861-6500

Million Dollar Round Table
2340 River Road
Des Plaines, IL 60018
(312) 298-1120

National Association of Bank
Women
500 North Michigan Avenue,
Suite 1400
Chicago, IL 60611
(312) 661-1700

American Society of Professional
   Estimators
5201 North Seventh Street,
   Suite 200
Phoenix, AZ 85014
(602) 274-4880

Building Owners and Managers
   Association International
1221 Massachusetts Avenue, NW
Washington, DC 20005
(202) 638-2929

Financial Executives Institute
633 Third Avenue
New York, NY 10017
(212) 953-0500

Independent Insurance Agents of
   America, Inc.
100 Church Street
New York, NY 10007
(212) 285-4250

Institute of Certified Financial
   Planners
3443 S. Galena, Suite 190
Denver, CO 80231
(303) 751-7600

National Association of Professional Insurance Agents
400 North Washington Street
Alexandria, VA 22314
(703) 836-9340

National Association of Realtors
430 North Michigan Avenue
Chicago, IL 60611
(312) 440-8000

National Security Traders
   Association
One World Trade Center
New York, NY 10048
(212) 524-0484

Securities Industry Association
20 Broad Street
New York, NY 10005
(212) 425-2700

Society of Real Estate Appraisers
645 North Michigan Avenue
Chicago, IL 60611
(312) 346-7422

LEISURE, TOURISM, AND TRAVEL

American Association of Leisure
   & Recreation
1900 Association Drive
Reston, VA 22091
(703) 476-3400

National Campground Owners
   Association
804 D Street, NE
Washington, DC 20002
(202) 543-6260

American Hotel and Motel
Association
888 Seventh Avenue
New York, NY 10019
(212) 265-4506

American Society of Travel
Agents
4400 MacArthur Boulevard
Washington, DC 20007
(202) 965-7520

National Recreation and Park
Association
3101 Park Center Drive
Alexandria, VA 22302
(703) 820-4940

Travel Industry Association of
America
1899 L Street, NW, Suite 600
Washington, DC 20036
(202) 293-1433

MANUFACTURING

American Association of Meat
Processors
224 East High Street, PO Box 269
Elizabethtown, PA 17022
(717) 367-1168

American Textile Manufacturers
Institute
1101 Connecticut Avenue, NW,
Suite 300
Washington, DC 20036
(202) 862-0500

Apparel Manufacturers
Association, Inc.
1440 Broadway
New York, NY 10018
(212) 398-0770

Chemical Manufacturers
Association
2501 M Street, NW
Washington, DC 20037
(202) 887-1100

Farm Equipment Manufacturers
Association
230 South Bemiston
St. Louis, MO 63105
(314) 725-5532

Industrial Fabrics Association
International
345 Cedar Building, Suite 450
St. Paul, MN 55101
(612) 222-2508

National Association of
Manufacturers
1776 F Street, NW
Washington, DC 20006
(202) 626-3700

National Hardwood Lumber
Association
Box 34518
Memphis, TN 38184
(901) 377-1818

PROFESSIONAL

American Bar Association
1155 East 60th Street
Chicago, IL 60637
(312) 947-4000

American Institute of Certified
    Public Accountants
1211 Avenue of the Americas
New York, NY 10036
(212) 575-6200

American Institute of Architects
1735 New York Avenue, NW
Washington, DC 20006
(202) 626-7300

American Society of Women
    Accountants
35 East Wacker Drive
Chicago, IL 60601
(312) 341-9078

Independent Computer
    Consultants
Box 27412
St. Louis, MO 63141
(314) 567-9708

Institute of Management
    Consultants
19 West 44th Street
New York, NY 10036
(212) 921-2885

Association of Management
    Consultants
500 North Michigan Avenue,
    Suite 1400
Chicago, IL 60611
(312) 661-1700

National Association of
    Accountants
919 Third Avenue
New York, NY 10022
(212) 754-9700

National Society of Public
    Accountants
1010 North Fairfax Street
Alexandria, VA 22314
(703) 549-6400

Professional Engineers in Private
    Practice
2029 K Street, NW
Washington, DC 20006
(202) 463-2300

SMALL BUSINESS

American Business Women's
    Association
P.O. Box 8728
9100 Ward Parkway
Kansas City, MO 64114
(816) 361-6621

International Council for Small
    Business
St. Louis University
3674 Lindell Boulevard
St. Louis, MO 63108
(314) 658-3826

American Chamber of Commerce
Executives
1133 15th Street, NW, Suite 620
Washington, DC 20005
(202) 296-1762

American Federation of Small
Business
407 South Dearborn Street
Chicago, IL 60605
(312) 427-0206

American Association of Small
Research Companies
8794 West Chester Pike
Upper Darby, PA 19082
(215) 449-2333

Center for Small Business
U.S. Chamber of Commerce
1615 H Street, NW
Washington, DC 20062
(202) 463-5503

National Business League
4324 Georgia Avenue, NW
Washington, DC 20011
(202) 829-5900

National Federation of
Independent Business
150 West 20th Avenue
San Mateo, CA 94403
(415) 341-7441

National Small Business
Association
1604 K Street, NW
Washington, DC 20006
(202) 296-7400

U.S. Hispanic Chamber of
Commerce
829 Southwest Boulevard
Kansas City, MO 64108
(816) 842-2255

RETAILING

American Booksellers Association
122 East 42nd Street
New York, NY 10168
(212) 867-9060

American Retail Federation
1616 H Street, NW
Washington, DC 20006
(202) 783-7971

Food Marketing Institute
1750 K Street, NW, Suite 700
Washington, DC 20006
(202) 452-8444

National Home Furnishing
Association
405 Merchandise Mart Plaza
Chicago, IL 60654
(312) 836-0777

National Independent Automobile
Dealers Association
3700 National Drive, Suite 208
Raleigh, NC 27612
(919) 781-2350

National Restaurant Association
311 First Street
Washington, DC 20001
(202) 638-6100

Jewelers of America, Inc.
1271 Avenue of the Americas,
　Suite 650
New York, NY 10020
(212) 498-0023

National Association of Chain
　Drug Stores
PO Box 1417-D49
Alexandria, VA 22313
(703) 549-3001

National Association of
　Convenience Stores, Inc.
Three Skyline Place, Suite 809
5201 Leesburg Pike
Falls Church, VA 20041
(703) 578-1800

National Association of Retail
　Druggists
205 Daingerfield Road
Alexandria, VA 22314
(703) 683-8200

National Retail Hardware
　Association
770 North High School Road
Indianapolis, IN 46224
(317) 248-1261

Retail Bakers of America
6525 Belcrest Road, Suite 250
Hyattsville, MD 20782
(301) 277-0990

Shoe Service Institute of America
154 West Hubbard Street
Chicago, IL 60610
(312) 236-2283

National Retail Merchants
　Association
100 West 31st Street
New York, NY 10001
(212) 244-8780

WHOLESALING

Durable Goods

Automotive Warehouse
　Distributors Association
9140 Ward Parkway, Suite 200
Kansas City, MO 64114
(816) 444-3500

Farm Equipment Wholesalers
　Association
PO Box 1347
Iowa City, IA 52240
(319) 354-5156

National Building Material
　Distributors
1701 Lake Avenue, Suite 170
Glen View, IL 60025
(312) 724-6900

Linen Trade Association
11 West 42nd Street
New York, NY 10036
(212) 944-2230

National Association of
Wholesaler-Distributors
1725 K Street, NW
Washington, DC 20006
(202) 872-0885

National Association of Electrical
Distributors
600 Summer Street
Stamford, CT 06901
(203) 327-1290

National Tire Dealers and
Retreaders Association, Inc.
1250 Eye Street, NW
Washington, DC 20005
(202) 789-2300

National Wholesale Furniture
Association
PO Box 1792
Highpoint, NC 27261
(919) 889-6411

Nondurable Goods

Grain Elevator and Processing
Society
Box 15024, Commerce Station
Minneapolis, MN 55415
(612) 339-4626

National Association of Tobacco
Distributors
630 Third Avenue, 17th Floor
New York, NY 10017
(212) 599-3344

National Wine Distributors
Association
101 East Ontario Street, Suite 760
Chicago, IL 60611
(312) 951-8878

United Fresh Fruit & Vegetable
Association
North Washington and Madison
Alexandria, VA 22314
(703) 836-3410

PUBLIC POLICY

National Governors Association
Hall of States
444 N. Capitol Street, NW,
Suite 250
Washington, DC 20001
(202) 624-5300

National League of Cities
1301 Pennsylvania Avenue, NW
Washington, DC 20004
(202) 626-3000

State Governmental Affairs
Council
1001 Connecticut Avenue, NW,
Suite 800
Washington, DC 20036
(202) 659-7605

U.S. Conference of Mayors
1620 Eye Street, NW
Washington, DC 20006
(202) 293-7330

RESPONDING TO RFPs

L ARGER ORGANIZATIONS and local state and federal government issue request for proposals (RFPs) to which a large number of competing firms may respond. Especially in the case of federal government contract proposals, you have reduced flexibility in determining the scope of work, level of effort, and presentation. You must be able to follow the required format and content prescribed by the contracting agency.

In preparation of writing a solicited proposal, five basic steps must be taken:

1. Analyze the RFP for the technical requirements of the job. (Few bidders do this.) Carefully observe any timing, sequencing, logistics, reporting, or other requirements. Also, fully familiarize yourself with the evaluation criteria: you must score high to win.

2. Make detailed notes of any inconsistencies or problems you may encounter in reading and interpreting the RFP. These should be resolved before writing the proposal. Feel free to call the designated agency official or contracting officer to discuss these problems. **201**

3. In all cases attempt to make personal contact with the agency or organization. Despite the stipulation that you should not make personal contact, touch base with agency officials who may be taking part in the initial review or with key staff members. It certainly helps if you are known. Try to elicit information on what type of firm the agency is seeking and how the job should be done.

4. Conduct background research on the problem, and review the goal of the agency or organization. A good source when bidding on federal contracts is the *Catalog of Federal Domestic Assistance*, which is offered on a subscription basis through the Office of Management and Budget, Executive Office of the President, Washington, DC 20503. State and local governments may have similar documents available. Be sure to inquire.

5. Contact any "neutral" individuals working in the content area for information they may be able to provide. This might include individuals within the specific agency or organization who have responsibility in some other program area. Whenever information about the agency or organization is obtained, it is of potential value to your proposal writing effort.

MECHANICS FOR WRITING

It is best to write a detailed outline of the entire proposal. A checklist for the mechanics of writing the proposal writing is presented in Exhibit 39.

EXHIBIT 39 MECHANICS OF PROPOSAL WRITING

Develop a checklist to ensure that all desired information is included

Use no more than four (4) indentations, for example:

   I. Section   (1)
      A. Subsection   (2)
         1. Topic   (3)
            a. Subtopic   (4)

Make sure that no one section is more than three (3) times the length (number of pages) of any other sections

Begin each new section on the top of a new page

Put the complete table of contents, exhibits, and appendix lists in the front of the proposal

Use spacing to facilitate reading

Attempt to limit lists to six (6) items, and at maximum nine (9) items

Include exhibits in the text adjacent to where the exhibit is referred

Tell the readers what you're going to say, state what you want to say, and tell them what you've said

Avoid acronyms, abbreviations, and colloquialisms; write to an uninformed audience who has moderate interest

Limit sentence length

Use graphs and charts freely, but make sure that they are able to stand alone

---

Also for each "we will do" statement that you make, add a corresponding "you will receive" benefit. This will help the proposal reviewer to follow your proposed approach.

REVIEWING THE PROPOSAL

When the proposal draft is completed, reviewers who have not taken part in the writing of the proposal should closely read, edit, and critique the proposal.

Checklists should now be used to determine whether the proposal addresses the issues and contains all the information that the proposal writers originally intended to include.

After the proposal is in A-1 shape and ready to be submitted, *review it again!*

SUBMITTING THE PROPOSAL

In general, submit the finished proposal in advance of the deadline. This is advantageous for several reasons, including the following:

1. Your proposal may stand out more clearly than those received during the last-minute avalanche.
2. Your proposal stands a better chance of being reviewed more fully.
3. Your peace of mind can be maintained.
4. You have effectively saved time and expense through early submission.

When responding to requests for proposals, always use plain paper and simple binding—nothing elaborate. Avoid fancy type or format. When submitting the proposal to the agency be sure to obtain a receipt.

About 7 to 10 days after submission, call to make sure that everything is in order and ask whether you can be of further assistance.

EXTRA WORKSHEET CHARTS

For: _____

(Service)

Your task is to identify client needs and problem situations for which your service is appropriate. For each verb listed below, identify how your service applies. For example, under the word "eliminate" you might put "unnecessary forms and procedures."

Improve or Enhance	Reduce, Relieve, or Eliminate
Protect	Restructure
Identify	Restore or Resolve

THREE-YEAR FINANCIAL PERFORMANCE

Year	Revenue, $ U.S.	Growth, %
198＿	_____	_____
198＿	_____	_____
198＿	_____	_____

THREE-YEAR DISTRIBUTION OF PERSONAL HOURS

Activity Areas	19____	19____	19____
Chargeable client work	_____	_____	_____
Marketing and practice development	_____	_____	_____
Other activities	_____	_____	_____
Total	_____	_____	_____

EXISTING "A" CLIENTS

Client	Assessment					Fees					Remarks
	RS	PS	PT	QOR	Industry	Latest 12 Months	Percentage of Total, %	Estimated Next 12 Months			
								Hours	$		

EXISTING "B" CLIENTS

Client	Assessment				Fees					Remarks
	RS	PS	PT	QOR	Industry	Latest 12 Months	Percentage of Total, %	Estimated Next 12 Months		
								Hours	$	

Client	Type		Fees			Industry	Remarks
	"C"	"D"	Latest 12 Months	Percentage of Total, %	Estimated Next 12 Months		
			$_____ total		$_____ total		

CURRENT PRIMARY AND SECONDARY MARKETS

Market	Percentage of Revenue, %	Description of Market	Potential for Growth Short Term	Long Term
		Current Primary Markets		
1.				
2.				
3.				
4.				
5.				
6.				
7.				
8.				
		Current Secondary Markets		
1.				
2.				
3.				
4.				
5.				
6.				
7.				
8.				

CLIENTS ACQUIRED/LOST SUMMARY

Start date			Present date		
Clients Acquired			Clients Lost		
Source	Number	Fees	Reasons	Number	Fees
Client referrals	_____	$ _____	Fee complaint	_____	$ _____
Leads from			Service complaint	_____	$ _____
recommendations	_____	$ _____	Moved out of		
Drop-ins/image	_____	$ _____	market	_____	$ _____
Targeted, self-			Merger or		
initiated action	_____	$ _____	acquisition	_____	$ _____
Advertising	_____	$ _____	Bankruptcy	_____	$ _____
Unknown	_____	$ _____	Outside pressure		
			Bank	_____	$ _____
			Government	_____	$ _____
			Sale of business	_____	$ _____
			Unknown	_____	$ _____

CLIENT REFERRAL SOURCES

Name, Title, and Organization	Quality of Relationship (1 to 5)	What Sources of New Business Does (S)He Represent?	How Do I Plan to Use this Referral Source?

TARGETS OF INFLUENCE

Names and Affiliations of Influential Contacts	QOR (1 to 5)	How Do I Plan to Effectively Use My Relationship with These People?

INDEX